Approaching the End:
Apocalyptic Vision in Graham Greene's Select Novels

Approaching the End:

Apocalyptic Vision in Graham Greene's Select Novels

Tasleem A War

ADHYAYAN

ADHYAYAN PUBLISHERS & DISTRIBUTORS

New Delhi-110002

Published by
ADHYAYAN PUBLISHERS & DISTRIBUTORS
4378/4B, 105, J.M.D. House, Murari Lal Street
Ansari Road Darya Ganj, New Delhi - 110002
Ph.: 011-23263018, 011-23277156, Fax: 23280028
Email: adhyayanpublishers@yahoo.com

Approaching the End:
Apocalyptic Vision in Graham Greene's Select Novels

Edition 2012
ISBN 978-81-8435-346-4

Printed in India

Published by Harish Chandra Yadav for Adhyayan Publishers & Distributors, Delhi. Laser Typesetting at Jain Computers and Printed at Tarun Offset Printers, Delhi

*For My Family with
Love and Gratitude*

Preface

Images of the end of the world abound in both American and British twentieth century literature. There are many demonic and secular manifestations of apocalypse like the all pervading sense of loss, doom, destruction, meaninglessness, breakdown of all systems, topsy turvy state of affairs and the sense of an ending which characterize the literature of the times. In British Literature, the writers like D H Lawrence and William Golding give expression to these satanic tendencies of the end times in their works. However the most important factors which shaped the vision of these writers are the two world wars which simply added fuel to the fire. The bug of apocalypse started biting everybody with the increasing impending sense of doom which loomed large in its horizons. James Joyce, William Butler Yeats and Joseph Conrad also give expression to this sense of futility and crisis in their peculiar ways. The book therefore makes an attempt to situate Graham Greene in both the biblical and secular socio-political tradition of the apocalypse as his writings are full of the signs of the end times. The book also highlights the similarities and dissimilarities of Greene's apocalyptic vision from all the other aforementioned writers.

In writing this book, I owe a lot to Professor Mohammad Aslam, Professor Pashupati Jha, Professsor G K Das, Professor Harish Narang, and Dr Rajni Singh whose insightful suggestions paved a way for me to prepare a final draft of this book. My thanks are also due to all those associated with The American Library, New Delhi, EFL University and OUCIP Hyderabad. It is with the help of the books which I got from all these libraries that I have been able to accomplish this task. Last of all I thank Mr. Harish for making all the required changes and help me to get this book published in his publishing house.

Tasleem A War

Contents

Introduction
Keyboard to the Exposition

Graham Greene is undoubtedly one of the major twentieth century British novelists. His stature as a novelist is attested by the ever increasing corpus of critique on his works that discuss his literary concerns, artistic merits and the overall contribution to the English novel. Critics on Greene have tended to highlight some of the main concerns of the novelist, and there have been attempts to present him as a catholic, an existentialist, a humanist, a socialist and even as an atheist.

The present study argues that Greene's works can be best understood as expressions of literary apocalypse and therefore presents apocalypse as the standard of reference with which to explain Greene's novels. Greene's novels can be termed as apocalyptic because of his predominant thematic concerns such as the fallen state of man, progressive degeneration, breakdown of all social set-ups and all value systems, nuclear warfare, two World Wars and, above all, his apocalyptic settings. Many of his works are set against the background of wars like the Spanish Civil War, the II World War, the Vietnam War etc. The destruction and bloodshed caused by these wars terribly shocked Greene, and they continued to haunt him and shaped his artistic vision. The title of one of the novels, *It is a Battlefield* could be taken as an epigraph to all his novels as the idea of destruction and desolation pervades his works sometimes directly and sometimes in the form of apocalyptic seedy settings and themes. The novels like *The Ministry of Fear, A Gun for Sale, Brighton Rock, The Power and the Glory, The Human Factor, A Burnt-out Case, The Heart of the Matter, The End of the Affair,* and even his short stories like *The Destructors* share certain common features that help to situate them against an apocalyptic background. In all these novels, there are unmistakable signs of disintegration of all social, political and even religious systems characteristic of the modern age. Apocalyptic settings often present a conflict between good and evil where the evil triumphs and the state of man is shown as irredeemable. As an apocalyptic novelist Greene is preoccupied with conflicts and clashes between various systems occurring at all levels. What stands out prominently, though, in these novels is Greene's inability or unwillingness to move beyond these preoccupations to a point where he can resolve this chaos and disintegration into some kind of meaningful end. His vision as a novelist is thoroughly dystopian, one informed by a sense of ineluctable doom that is bound to engulf all mankind. His artistic sensibility despite its iintimate links with his catholic faith is unable to resolve the paradox he finds himself in. Greene's paradox lies in his position as a catholic novelist who is constantly forced to foresee nothing but the march of humanity towards the ultimate doom where even religion and adherence to his teachings, offer little hope for regeneration. Greene is, thus, caught up in the dilemma between affirmation and negation. Despite his avowed catholic faith, his artistic vision is informed by a thorough going pessimism. This becomes clear when Greene's heroes such as the Whisky priest, Scobie, Sarah etc are seen as heroes whose sacrifice can at best earn them their personal salvation. It seems that these novels are irredeemably bleak and none of them ends on a note of promise or hope.

Greene's novels bear witness to his perennial interest in metaphysical questions like God, morality, conduct etc.

But Greene, more than anything else, is a novelist who is prominently interested in man. Man is the subject of almost all his novels. How, then, does Greene conceptualize man? Man, for Greene, possesses irreducible qualities; he is a social, ethical and emotional creature, it is often said that Greene moves beyond the strict dogmatism of religious faith to affirm human values. The point, howsoever valid, must not be allowed to obscure the fact that his affirmation of these human values, independent of religious faith, raises certain questions about his final vision. If Christian love can be interpreted entirely in human terms, what then is the status of dogma and faith? It seems plausible to maintain that the best guide to Greene's creative works is his definition of himself as a Catholic Atheist. The paradox of this oxymoron is more than superficial. It explains the fact that Greene is constantly struggling between the two pulls of Catholic affirmation and atheistic negation and his artistic vision is borne out of this unresolved conflict. The works of Greene are marked by a curious appropriation of both the catholic and aesthetic elements in his art.

The curious blend of faith and its negation provides the key for seeing Greene as an apocalyptic writer *par excellence.* In fact his conversion to Catholic faith, the present study argues, is largely due to his recognition that of all Christian denominations, Catholicism affords central importance to evil. The metaphysical evil which is an integral part of Catholic outlook often manifests itself in disease, destruction, war and other evils, themes that have obsessed Greene's imagination throughout his career. The paradox, however, remains at its place as Catholicism, like many other Christian and even non-Christian systems, upholds the ultimate victory of good over evil. Greene, however, foresees no such possibility and hence affirms a Catholicism strongly compromised by an antithetical strain. It is these concerns of Greene that have been dealt with in this study.

The first chapter entitled "Perspectivising Apocalyptic

Literature" presents a brief overview of apocalypse, tracing its religious origin and development through certain important historical junctures. It also discusses the significance of the secular apocalypse and how it came to be used in literature by different critics. The second chapter entitled "Graham Greene and the Passages to Epiphany" presents certain important biographical details about Greene's childhood experiences that finally shaped his vision as a novelist. In this chapter, a detailed discussion of Greene's Catholic faith is undertaken to validate the assertion that Catholicism made an indelible imprint on his sensibility but this import found manifestation in themes that are apocalyptic. The third chapter entitled "Dark Clouds & Graham Greene" analyses those novels of Greene in which he deals with the brutal reality of several wars and their adverse consequences. This chapter also aims to highlight the suffering and the destruction caused by wars which preoccupied the mind of Greene and shaped his dystopic vision. The novels analyzed in this chapter are: The *Ministry of Fear, The Quiet American,* and some minor novels, essays and also his stories. Chapter four entitled "Backdrop to Structural Forms" attempts to analyze those novels of Greene in which he directly does not deal with war reality but highlights the obsessive nature of Greene with seedy settings and the themes like death, murder, emptiness and rootlessness of life, the fallen state of humanity which is caught up in the aboriginal calamity and the breakdown of traditional systems. This is followed by "Epilogue" which attempts to sum up what has already been said in the preceding chapters and also highlight its overall status and picture that emerges out of this particular reading of Greene.

1

Perspectivising Apocalyptic Literature

The term apocalypse has been in use for a long time. Its usage in religious and literary discourses has, however, not been without certain obstacles as far as its meaning and scope are concerned. The word 'apocalypse' as is well known has a religious origin. It has been derived from the Greek word "apocalypse" which means "to remove the cover from (to uncover) or (to reveal)". It is in the last book of *The Bible, The Revelation,* that apocalypse, signifying the end of the world, finds its full expression. *The Book of Revelation,* also called *Revelation to John* or *Apocalypse of John* is the last canonical book of the *New Testament* in *The Bible* and the only biblical book that is wholly composed of apocalyptic literature.

The word apocalypse has many meanings. As mentioned earlier, in religious usage, it identifies the last book of the Christian Bible, *The Revelation of John;* a genre of ancient Judo-Christian visionary literature; or doomsday, the destruction of the world at the end of time prophesied by the apocalypse. Apocalyptism is a religious belief system that interprets human history from its origin to the present as signs of the imminent end of the world. It is one feature of Christian eschatology, the branch of theology dealing with the state of the soul after death, purgatory, hell and heaven. Apocalypticism is a feature of all three monotheistic religions. *The Book of Daniel* describes the Hebrew Prophet's vision of the end. In Islam, the resurrection, the Day of Judgment and salvation are apocalyptic features of orthodox belief as evident in the *Quran.* J.J.Collins, as a part of the Society of Biblical Literature's 1970s commission to systematically analyze apocalyptic literature of both Jewish and Christian origins, cites the resulting collaborative definition in the following manner:

> An apocalypse is a genre of revelatory literature with a narrative framework in which a revelation is mediated by another worldly being to a human recipient, disclosing a transcendent reality which is both temporal, in so far as it envisages eschatological salvation, and spatial, in so far as it involves another, supernatural world.[1]

Apocalypticism, however, is common in Christianity, probably because of the continuing influence of the biblical Apocalypse, which has informed not only the eschatology of Christianity but also in art, literature and worship. Its rich, otherworldly symbolism and prophecies of the end of time are well-known and include the four Horsemen, lamb of god, Mark of the beast (666), Armageddon, last judgment and New Jerusalem, Apocalyptic writing is that which aims to reveal or disclose something hidden. The strongest association of the word is with the *Book of Revelation.* Apocalypse in the Christian bible uncovers vision of future chaos at the end of time. The Inaugural signs of the apocalypse, as described in *The Revelation,* shall be occasional natural disturbances like earthquakes and floods followed by most turbulent reign of the Antichrist, This is called the Armageddon, cosmic warfare, which shall result in the inauguration of the millennium or the Messianic Kingdom. A gradual moral and physical degeneration of human nature will set in as the rule of the Messiah is over. This total degeneration of human nature will be characterized by the last loosening of Satan, to be followed by the ultimate catastrophe-the end of the world by fire. Finally comes the judgment, followed by gods making of a new heaven and earth[2]. The Hindu doctrine teaches that the human cycle called *Manvantara* is divided into four periods. These periods correspond with the Golden, Silver, Bronze and Iron Ages of the ancient western traditions. It is believed that we are now in the fourth age, the *Kali-Yuga* or Dark Age. In this Dark Age, cyclic development proceeds in a downward direction, from higher to lower, a course which appears to be perceived to be the complete antithesis of the idea of progress as understood by the moderns. This fall might be described as progressive materialization. The real starting point of the modern crisis dates from that point. What people call Renaissance was actually the death of many things. On the pretext of a return to Greece-Roman civilization it merely took over the most outward part of that civilization. In literature, modernism started with the Renaissance, which has been defined differently by different critics. Harold Rosenbarg defines modern art as "the tradition of the new"[3] which can also be understood as the artist's freedom from realism, materialism, traditional genre and form, with notions of cultural apocalypse and disaster and decadence. Looking at modernism as a timeless concept, Modernism has its genesis in the Renaissance which meant rebirth, revival and volcanic eruption of the learning of ancient Greece and Rome. Actually it was a revival of everything but the spirit. It also led to a shift from god-centric world to man-centric world, As a Time bound concept-1890-1930-the best focus remains a body of major writers- James, Conrad, Proust, Mann, Gide, Kafka, Svevo, Joyce, Musil and Faulkner in fiction; Strindberg, Pirandello, Wedekind and Brecht in drama; Mallarme, Yeats, Eliot, Pound, Rilke, Apollinaire and Stevens in poetry—whose works involve a certain "dehumanization of art."[4] With regard to literature, Modernism is best understood through the work of the Modernist authors who wrote in the decades before and after the turn of the twentieth century. All modem European literature, particularly since World War I, responds to a world that seemed to be falling apart and becoming increasingly meaningless in the wake of the brutal advance of capitalism, rampant individualism and the consequent loss of community, large-scale devastation of the world wars, threat of a nuclear holocaust, and the destruction of the liberal traditions of hope and faith in man's innate goodness, rationality and progress. These writings, their individual richness notwithstanding, can be broadly classified, in terms of their world views and ideological orientations into three categories. One, the mythico-religious response which was exemplified by writers like W B Yeats and T S Eliot, which sees hope only in a revival of religious faith and spiritual values, thus implying an escape into some glorified past or transcendental realm from the horrors of the present. Two, the historical materialist response which was best exemplified in Bertolt Brecht, Mayakovsky, Bernard Shaw and Sean O'Casey, which tries to analyse and understand the existing situation historically and, asserting the changeability of the world, stresses the possibility and desirability of turning it into a happier place through collective effort. The third kind of response is what may be described as a subjective and idealist response that contemplates the world in abstract philosophical terms and finds it not only unchanging but also unchangeable. It usually ends up accepting meaninglessness, loneliness and disintegration as the permanent and universal condition of human existence itself.

Modernity as a part of apocalypse pinpoints a moment of potential breakdown in socio-cultural relations and aesthetic representation, which gave rise to a general feeling of anxiety. This may not have followed from Spengler's book[5] but for many historical and political reasons it has become a widespread anxiety among creative artists, economists, political thinkers from around the turn of the century. Frank Kermode has aptly called this anxiety "The sense of an Ending"[6] and Watson calls it "The Myth of Catastrophe." [7] Kermode says further, "Apocalypse is a part of the modern absurd."[8] Modernism can also be taken as a response by artists and writers to several things, including industrialization, urban society, war, technological change and new philosophical ideas. Because the nineteenth century experienced a spreading disillusionment with existing models of the individual and the social, the Western world was transformed and reinterpreted by Marx, Freud and Darwin,[9] who respectively changed established notions of the social, the individual and the natural. Imperialism had exposed European sensibilities to alternative cultures, ethics and social structures. World War I and the years immediately before and after it, brought about the destruction of many institutions and beliefs; the class system was rocked by the rise of trade unions and the Labor Party; beliefs in King and Country, patriotism and duty were betrayed by the carnage of the war. In terms of the trauma of the war itself, the effect on modern consciousness cannot be overstated. It resulted in the invention of new weapons, such as submarines, airplanes, poisonous gas and cannons with a range over 75 miles. It also produced more than 33 million military casualties, and an additional 5 million civilian deaths, not counting the millions of war related influenza deaths. With devastation of such a scale, it became absurd to celebrate noble ideas like human dignity in art, or blithely to assert a belief in human progress. The war produced a deep distrust of optimistic secular or teleological understandings of history, and it seemed a climactic and severing event that showed conclusively the failures of the nineteenth century rationalism. The war was a defining moment in terms of both society and the individual, such that the fracturing of minds that came to be known as shell-shock seemed to represent in miniature what was happening to societies and nations, as much of the world went to war, Europe was torn apart, and Russia thrown into revolution. William Butler Yeats in one of his famous poems *The Second Coming,* (1919) reveals the horror vision of the destruction of the world in these words:

> Turning and turning in the widening gyre
> The falcon cannot hear the falconer;
> Things fall apart; the center cannot hold;
> Mere anarchy is loosed upon the world...
> Surely some revelation is at hand;
> Surely the Second Coming is at hand.
> The second coming![10]

The opening lines of the poem give us a picture of the disintegration which has overtaken the Christian civilization. Things are falling apart, and there is no stabilizing force. Lawlessness and confusion are spreading over the world. The indications are that some new revelation or a new "coming" is near. The Christian civilization is disintegrating, and a new epoch will begin. This new epoch, however, is fraught with evil and wickedness. All great modern literature exhibits unmistakable apocalyptic tendencies as in the works of Conrad and Golding who were especially interested in depicting apocalyptic themes in their novels. Joseph Conrad's *Heart of Darkness* represents an early modern manifesto in the direction of the apocalypse. We can detect Conrad's tug towards the eschatological, which means towards the image of final universal dissolution. William Golding who lived through the two world wars had the personal experience of what a war does to human society. The background of his novel[11] is a nuclear warfare in Europe. The message of this novel is that man is essentially a creature of wild passions and inherent evils. Civilization cannot change him basically. Hidden evil tendencies may crop up at any moment. Thus, Golding explodes the myth of progress and belief in science. The human struggle between faith and doubt and the despair and alienation of modern humanity are constant themes in his work.

The modem apocalyptic imagination in contemporary literature is secular because it actually reflects the demonic aspects of the apocalyptic world of the Bible in secular terms. Modem man's secular imagination pictures an apocalypse of despair, in which the end of the world will be final, without the promise of any renewal. No new heaven or earth will follow. A sense of helplessness and despair envisioned about the future of man are *final* and total.

Apocalyptic literature has some basic characteristics. It deals with secret or hidden information which can only be disclosed by supernatural means through dreams or visions from god or angelic intermediaries. The message of apocalyptic literature is communicated in mysterious, enigmatical forms through the use of bizarre, often-times obscure symbolism and imagery. Its fantastic world of beasts, signs, colors, numbers and angels seems to have functioned as a type of code which effectively communicated its message to a secret group while concealing the message from the uninitiated.

Apocalyptic literature finds expression in literature either through Utopia or Dystopia. Both utopian and dystopian writers have the same end in their minds but they approach it differently. In utopian writing, the writer ends on a note of hope, thus leaving a scope for the establishment of an ideal society. The dystopian writer on the contrary, offers/envisions a completely pessimistic picture of the world, without any renewal or hope. When it is pessimistic, there is little possibility for progress or positive development within the normal framework of human endeavour. From the dystopian apocalyptic point of view, things are bad and they are only going to get worse as far as men are concerned. This literature is written in times of catastrophic change as previously well-ordered world views collapse. Apocalyptic writers see themselves in the midst of the catastrophic destruction of a way of life, even of the entire universe. The utopian apocalyptic writers, on the other hand, proceed on the firm conviction that in his own good times, God will intervene to bring the evil of this world to an end and proclaim His ultimate victory. It has been aptly described as the anticipatory raising of the curtain to display the final scene. It is, in a way, conveying pictorially and symbolically the conviction of the ultimate victory of God. In recent times, the term apocalypse has been used to refer to that kind of literature which incorporates certain dominant features of the apocalypse discussed above. Critics have identified apocalypse in genres such as *science fiction.*

The primary and basic feature of the secular or demonic apocalypse consists in showing contemporary civilization as passing through a phase corresponding to the last loosening of Satan, which in *The Revelation* just precedes the end. In contemporary fiction, the last loosening of Satan comes in different forms and under many different guises. Modern man's fondness for violence and destruction is considered to be symbolic of Satan's influence. Secular apocalypse is permeated with the images and themes from biblical writing, although a major departure from religious apocalypse is the emphasis on disaster as the primary interest in secular writing. Hence, the most popular use of the term apocalypse, which is used to mean not revelation but widespread destruction.

There are many writers in the twentieth century who have expressed their apocalyptic vision in their own peculiar way. All of them have their own distinct views about it. Nineteenth-century American novelists, such as, Nathanel Hawthorne, Herman Melville and Mark Twain were the first to reflect the apocalyptic imagination in its secular version in fiction, depicting Satan let loose in society. Hawthorne's *Blithedale Romance* (1852), Melville's *The Confidence Man* (1887), and Twain's *The Mysterious Stranger* (1916), each dwelt upon the degeneration of human morals under the influence of demonic tendencies in individuals as a prelude to a social disaster.

R.W.B.Lewis was the first among the contemporary critics of apocalyptic literature, to trace the genesis of apocalyptic imagination in contemporary fiction. In his book, he labels the secular version of apocalypse as Ludicrous Catastrophe[12] and traces its origin from *Melville's The Confidence Man* and *Twain's The Mysterious Stranger* to Nathanel West's *The Day of the Locust (*1939) and many other works of contemporary American novelists such as Ralph Ellison, Thomas Pynchon, John Barth and Joseph Heller. Lewis analyses the various interpretations of the last loosening of Satan, given by people in different centuries and finally discusses a few apocalyptic novels. John R.May takes up some of the insights of Lewis and works these out by focusing upon the use of the apocalyptic imagination in some modern American novels. May says that apocalypse "is a response to a cultural crisis."[13] He discusses the secular strain in apocalypse and remarks that the times immediately preceding the end are characterized by a general breakdown of moral standards, which explains the presence and acceptability of Satan in his many disguises.[14] And May links it with the advent of *Kali Yuga,* the evil age through which modern civilization is passing at present. He is of the opinion that contemporary literature is caught between hope and despair. David Ketterer advocates that apocalyptic thought is an inextricable component of much of science fiction today and that apocalyptic imagination finds its purest outlet in science fiction[15] which is defined as "the search for a definition of mankind and his status in the universe which will stand in our advanced but confused state of knowledge (science), and is characteristically cast in the Gothic or post-Gothic mode.[16]

In the light of above definition Mary Shelley's Frankenstein [17] is certainly the first great work of science fiction followed by *The Last Man,*[18] both present dystopic visions of alternative possibilities for the human race. Science fiction established itself as a major genre of popular contemporary fiction in the magazines of the 1920s and

1930s, in which Arthur C. Clarke, Isaac Asimov, and Robert Heinlein first published their stories. Science fiction is practically the only major literary form that deals with issues that arise from this: the Vietnam War, revolutions in evil society, radiation, environmental degradation, even over-population, robotics and the issues of automation verses unemployment. The food requirements of a growing human population, the consequent over-population of Earth's shrinking resources and possible alternative solutions, all feature in Science fiction. Ketterer defines three categories of apocalypse which overlap. These are "ecological apocalypse, biblical apocalypse and the science fictional philosophical apocalypse."[19] He also argues that an apocalyptic transformation results from the creation of a new condition.[20] Critics have identified the decades following World War II as a time when dystopic and apocalyptic visions of the world became dominant in a speculative work. Veronica Hollinger has suggested that much earlier "classic science fiction... is optimistic about the future of human beings"[21] which Paul Brains notes that science fiction gradually became bleaker over time:

In the 1940s science fiction had promoted itself as prophetic and inspirational. In the 1950 it had been diagnostic and critical, but typically provided some sort of happy ending. But in the 1960s the dominant mood of much of the best writing could only be described as nihilistic. At last science fiction found a fictional voice appropriate to the nightmare of nuclear war.[22]

Frank Kermode in his *The Sense of an Ending* isolates "Terrors, Decadence and Revelation, Transition and Clerkly Skepticisms"[23] as aspects of apocalyptic thinking. He maintains that modern man is struck in the middle and goes on imagining or constructing fictive ends, as he has no sense of belonging either to the beginning or the end. Some scholars use apocalyptic as if it were a synonym for eschatology, the study of the end, of final things. The whole of Frank Kermode's book, *The Sense of an Ending,* follows that usage. The theme is belabored in Galbraith's description of apocalyptic concern with "the end of the world, the end of the human species, the end of the West, the end of the age."[24] McGinn distinguishes apocalyptic from general eschatology only by way of the former's sense of the proximity of the end. The conception about the true nature of modern secular apocalyptic thought or the demonic apocalypse becomes clear in Northop Frye.[25] The imagery of the apocalyptic world of the *Bible,* as discussed by Frye, consists of the divine, human, animal, vegetable and mineral worlds, In modern secular apocalypse, the five worlds of the biblical apocalypse get parodied in their nauseating and repulsive forms, creating demonic imagery of the heavenly world of the Bible. Modern novelists present the contemporary civilization in terms of this demonically parodied world. That is why Frye calls this type of parody of apocalyptic imagery as demonic imagery. In contemporary fiction, the demonic and the apocalyptic have become identical. Bernard Bergonzie has also talked about the genesis of an apocalyptic imagination in contemporary fiction:

> Since the second world war many novels have contained images of collective catastrophe, whether in conventional literary terms or as science fiction, dwelling on the horrors of totalitarianism, a third world war and nuclear devastation.[26]

Like Lewis, John R.May and others, Bernard Bergonzie subscribes to the view that current apocalyptic thought was mainly inspired by the catastrophic advent of World War II and its aftermath. R.Buckminster Fuller, speaking about the novel of an atomic extinction, says "that for every pound of human flesh there are 200 pounds of self-annihilating explosives"[27]

Michael Barkun says that the "apocalyptic myths of the last several decades" have concentrated upon a nuclear holocaust, an ecological disaster, over-population, and this is because technology and the expansion of international transactions have made all this possible.[28] Erich Fromm[29] is of the opinion that science and technology have made man a robot, a machine, whose reason deteriorates with increase in his intelligence. Man has thus got equipped with the greatest material power without the wisdom to use it creating thus a very dangerous situation. Richard A. Falk says that:

> Population pressure is growing, that the danger of nuclear war persists and is probably increasing, that various forms of pollution are impinging upon our environment...[30]

He labels the decade of the seventies as one of despair, the 1980s as the politics of desperation, 1990s as the politics of catastrophe and the twenty-first century as an era of annihilation. There are many writers who also emphasize upon the destruction of mankind through nuclear war, environmental pollution, and population growth. In his book *The Doomsday Syndrome,* John Maddox [31] expresses grave doubts about the future survival of mankind in view of man's own crimes. Science and technology are labelled as the Devil's tools. Robert Alter in an article entitled *The Apocalyptic temper* refers to the ideas of R W B Lewis regarding modern apocalyptic thought and says that the millennial gloom vanished from a vision of an apocalypse with the advent of contemporary times, "leaving only a brooding sense of the imminence of the end."[32] Quoting D H Lawrence, Alter also says that the Apocalypse...is repellent because it resounds with the dangerous snarl of the frustrated, suppressed collective self, the frustrated power-spirit in man, Vengeful.[33] Kenneth L Woodward, Angus Deming, and Judith Gingold are of the opinion that apocalyptic talk has become too common: It used to be felt that the only people who cared about doomsday were fundamental preaches who paddled gloom as if they owned a piece of the Apocalypse. Today, however, Americans can hardly pick up a newspaper or magazine, tune in a talk show or go to a movie that does not trumpet disaster.[34] The author furnished a relevant reason for this:

functions in Aldous Huxley's *Time must Have a Stop,* William Golding's *Darkness Visible* and Don Delillo's *White Noise* we are better able to comprehend how prophetic presences within the latter novels affect reader perception and therefore affect the way in which we perceive and therefore receive modern apocalyptic literature. According to George Turner:

> .....the realities of overpopulation, ineradicable pollution, rampant nationalism and plain entrepreneurial greed the four horsemen of Greenhouse apocalypse- closed around the Planet. [38]

In the contemporary literature, the terms apocalypse and postmodern have been used interchangeably by many writers. Sometimes the two terms were used together as the 'postmodern apocalypse.' In *Postmodern Apocalypse,* Richard Dellamora writes of a pervasive sense of unease in contemporary existence. Arguing that the "lack of confidence in the possibility of shaping history in accord with human desire(s) provides the base line of culture, political, economic, and aesthetic." [39]

More than a decade after Dellamora's remarks, a collective dread evident in literature and film has not abated; rather, it has perhaps intensified. The real and immediate threat of a nuclear war was perhaps most prevalent in the years following 1945 and has since decreased, yet terrorist attacks throughout the world, as well as growing fears about global warming, have continued to provide impetus to the apocalyptic tradition. Particularly, in the wake of terrorist attacks on New York City in 2001 and London in 2005, it is perhaps no surprise that literature and film have featured a steady stream of apocalyptic scenarios. For instance, in a five year period after 2001 just some of the disaster films released include *The Core, The Day after Tomorrow,* the remake *Poseidon,* adaptations of novels such as *I, Robot and War of the Worlds,* and tale-movies including *Category 6: Day of Destruction, Category 1, The End of the World, Locusts: Day of Destruction, Oil Storm, Super Volcano, 10.5,* and *10.5: Apocalypse (1).*

Our era suffers the malaise of philosophical uncertainty causing a sense of urgency, as human beings have a tendency to want to reduce the tension and anxiety caused by uncertain and anxious situations as quickly as possible. Obviously, there is a range of possible responses to situations of increased tension. However, the human drive to reduce anxiety also surfaces in dramatic and revolutionary ways: intellectual revolutions, on the one hand, and millennial movements, on the other. The uncertain postmodern situations are illuminated by Western culture's propensity to make myths about end times. There are several characteristics common to both millennial movements and postmodern thought. In general terms, both anticipate the role of a crisis or disaster as something that upsets the usual order of things and instigates change. Moreover, both conclude that the traditional means of explaining the world are no longer adequate. Both also provide a new, revivalistic vision of the world; and finally, people of both the postmodern and apocalyptic ilk suffer from a specific degree of angst caused by the recognition of impending doom of civilization as they know it. In *The Passion of the Western Mind,* Richard Tarnas characterizes the postmodern condition as one that is subversive of all paradigms.[40] He explains that we can find at the core of postmodernity's style of criticism the awareness that reality is "at once multiple local and temporal and without demonstrable foundation."[41] Because we now understand reality as consisting of a multiple of dimensions that are all constructs of human symbol using and imaginative inclinations, we can no longer sustain any grand cosmological theories without producing "empirical and intellectual authoritarianism."[42]

One consequence of such relativization of all thought is that we can no longer theorise without being suspicious of our simplicity in reaffirming traditional world views that institutionalize and codify our selves. We live in a state of intellectual uncertainty and so it has become the task of many contemporary thinkers to develop an intellectual vision that accounts for the profound diversity of the world and humanity. There is the need of an intellectual revelation, an alternate paradigm that will provide sustainable and fertile ground for the "generation of unanticipated new perspectives and possibilities in the future."[43]

The elements belonging to the modern intellectual situation parallel those found in apocalyptic movements. To make the analogy more explicit, it is necessary to look at the conditions required for the emergence of apocalyptic visions which instigate millennial movements. Michael Barkum presents the following as a nutshell definition of millenarian movements:

> [They] are social movements which expect immediate, collective, total, this worldly salvation. They anticipate the complete destruction of the existing social order, political and economic order, which is to be superseded by a new and perfect society. They frequently couple this anticipation with an active desire to spread the inevitable result, often through violent, revolutionary means.[44]

This description sounds rather like deconstruction. Deconstruction proceeds from the assumption that traditional ways of viewing the world are wrong or false; it then delegitimises such metanarratives, thus leaving space open for the Postmodern Romantic impulse to speculate upon a brighter future. Disaster plays a role in bringing about a social change. Disasters upset social ordering of the world that surround a community. Moreover, disasters are not necessarily acts of God or of Nature. Man made disasters now proliferate, including economic instability, nuclear war, environmental catastrophe, political unrest, as well as ethical and intellectual deprivation. Other characteristics to millennial movements include:

> an intense emotional expression; the absolute condemnation of the existing political and social order,

> while denying its legitimacy, the transgression of accepted norms, laws, and taboos; and unrealistic aims in regard to the work of revitalizing society.[45]

Barkum analyzes American expressions of Apocalypticism between the 1960's and 1985 and states that an:

> apocalyptic chic has been accompanied by the emergence of political radicalism, a sense of ideological exhaustion... the simultaneous emergence of a new form of leftism in American culture...as well as a resurgence of fundamentalist perspectives and practices, and finally the appearance of secular apocalyptic literature.[46]

Briefly, the ten years following Kennedy's assassination have been seen as a period in which one perceived disaster emerging after another. Martin Luther King's death and the resulting race riots, Vietnam War, the advent of the new left radicals and the hippy dropouts, the emergence of Southern fundamentalism, to name a few. Moreover, there were social and legal changes that:

> helped prepare the way for a new millennium ambience: the women's movement, with its challenge to traditional gender roles; the increasing frequency of sex before and outside marriage; the visibility and activism of the gay community; and, supreme court decisions banning school prayer and permitting abortion.[47]

More interesting, however, is the concurrent rise in the influence of secular apocalyptic literature among intellectuals, government officials and business leaders. Examples of secular apocalypticism include such challenges as feminist thought, a perceived environmental disaster, scenarios regarding planetary destruction and certain Internet subcultures. By reinforcing the authority of apocalyptic themes, secular intellectuals helped make apocalyptic thought more acceptable in Western society as a whole. Moreover, there has been a trend in recent scholarship to acknowledge that apocalypticism is increasingly becoming a global phenomenon. Apocalypticism is now understood to be a phenomenon that transcends historical periods and cultures, and encompasses "the traditionally religious as well as the avowedly secular."[48]

Yet, as Barkun points out, there is also a romantic element in secular apocalypticism: the optimism that we will transcend Homosapiens and become Homo humanus.[49] Just as religious apocalyptic visions anticipate a new revitalized society emerging from the carcass of the past world, so too does contemporary of a pristine, more perfect society.

Statements like these lend credence to the fact that there is a similarity between apocalyptic and postmodern styles of thought. Disasters and threats of disasters during the past thirty years such as natural calamities, abortion, the gulf war, the AIDS epidemic, as well as political and economic instability throughout the world all contribute to our psychic condition as members of Western society. Because of the uncertainty and anxiety caused by this perceived string of disastrous events, those of them in the West may be suffering from what is called *disastrous syndrome.* This is a condition in which people become stunned, withdrawn, passive, and suggestible experience diminished mental capacity and have difficulties in perceiving reality correctly.[50]

It is the frequency of perceived disasters, their intensification via mass media, and the increasing acceptability of challenging and transgressing society's norms that places the postmodern perspectives firmly in the apocalyptic genre. Postmodern thought in many ways belongs to a genre which can be described as apocalyptic. Belief in objectivity is supplication to a modern myth that emerged during the Enlightenment. The very notion that there was even an age of reason or Enlightenment has mythic implications. Through deconstruction we might say that the postmodern world is in the process of re-mythologizing the stories which have emerged out of the legacy of Cartesian Newtonian thought and brought about the cosmology of modernity. Robert Brockway informs us:

> Both the enlightenment and deconstructionist positions are subjective interpretations rooted in the milieu of times, the personalities and psychologies of historians, and many other factors. For these reasons they are more like the myths, legends and story-telling of archaic times than they are not.[51]

This is to say that like paradigms and myths are founded on the best available evidence at any given time and "are discredited when the evidence no longer sustains them."[52] Brockway also suggests that when a specific myth no longer functions as an efficient theory or cosmology for a society, new ones rise to attention. Like Kuhn, Brockway claims that these "new" myths were already present as cultural artefacts because they emerged out of the old myths, "first us modifications and revisions, and ultimately as independent species, something new and different,"[53] These considerations about myths suggest two things: first, myth-making is an inherent human activity, we make myths in the sense that we invent paradigms and the major change in the modern age has been in the style of mythic expression, "the archaic myth is a metaphor; the modern myth is a theory. Both are models of paradigms."[54] Second, the myths or paradigms that we invent are invariably based upon dominant themes of our society. For Brockway, the reason that the apocalyptic genre is present in postmodern thought is that the myths upon which messianism or apocalypticism, for instances, are based "are detectable as the basic foundation on which Western society is built."[55]

The myths that Brockway believes to constitute the foundation to Western stories are the eternal return and the Hero who slays the dragon. According to the myth of eternal return, "there is neither an absolute beginning nor terminus, but instead, infinite regression in the past and eternal recurrence for all time to come."[56]

It is the myth that is more characteristic of ancient Greece, India and the East, than it is of the West since the onset of Judaism. However, the *Hebrews* completely reject the myth of the *Eternal Return* and conceive of history as the period between creation and judgment that ushers in an eternal divine order. Consequently, we can conclude that the Western Christian world view is one that is based, at least in part, in the apocalyptic vision symbolized by the hero who defeats chaos and recasts reality. So it is in the Hero who slays the dragon that we can find both postmodern and apocalyptic styles with past monsters and the vision of creating a new and better world. The apocalyptic postmodern hero is that would fight for the de-institutionalization of traditional social edifices, subvert traditional authority, and bring about a new and more perfect society. Consequently, we might say that the apocalyptic postmodern hero is optimistic and idealistic; faced with a disastrous contemporary situation.

There are many pamphleteers who would have the public believe that we are nearing the end of our culture, even of life on this planet as we know it and that the end of the world "is coming very soon, and you better be ready for it."[57] They hold the doomsday theory to be a realistic appraisal of today's situation. The approach of the year 2000 and the next millennium has put the fear of God into a good many people. "After we get into the 90s, we're going to see a lot more apocalyptic prophecy," [58] predicts J.Gordon Melton, the Director of the institute for the study of American Religion. The conviction that humans are living in the latter days is shared by millions of fundamentalist Christians. In fact, Whalen-Bridge argues that "by the late 1980s...the apocalyptic fundamentalists no doubt outnumber the members of the traditional (hard-core) end of the world sects."[59] The second, allusive mainstream forms of apocalyptic is that most likely to be espoused in public, especially by leaders in high places.

One is reminded of Ronald Reagan's antic secretary of the interior, James Watt, who justified a rapacious stance toward natural resources by arguing that we need to conserve them because Christ is coming soon anyway. Similarly, Reagan's Secretary of Defense, Caspar Weinberger, while no consistent apocalyptic seer, occasionally laced his public remarks with such observations as:

> I have read the book of revelations and, yes, I believe the world is going to end by an act of God, I hope-but every day, I think that time is running out.[60]

A third reason why today's apocalyptic discourse needs to be taken seriously is that the structure of religiously grounded apocalyptic also underlies a great deal of secular discourse. Secular apocalyptic also comes in systematic and allusive forms and because it follows the structure but not the content of the religious apocalyptic, it is limited in range while more varied in content. Many writers who warn of economic, ecological, civil or military disaster are employing a structure of argument that parallels systematic or allusive forms of religious apocalyptic exactly. Secular apocalyptic also includes socio-ecological and political alarms such as the exhaustion of the earth's natural resources, the pollution of air and sea.

There is, then, a kind of discourse having to do with the end of the world, with cataclysm and change that both energizes audiences and is used by many people and to call this discourse apocalyptic, or such terms as millennialism or eschatology, requires further clarification because the term apocalyptic is used in so many varying ways. Scheer argues that "many scholars use the term, but few define it carefully."[61] He also warns that the term apocalyptic may be extended too far, to cover too many kinds of discourse, "because scholars have been reluctant to explain precisely what they mean by the term."[62] Most of the contemporary critics use the term in the sense of disaster or crisis. This is surely the most popular usage, as reflected in popular culture artefacts such as Francis Ford Coppola's film *Apocalypse Now* and in a Rock Musician Prince's album 1999, the apocalyptic imagination is appropriated in two popular American films, *Wateworld* and *Twelve Monkeys.* In these two films we see that popular culture has taken a traditional religious concept of apocalypse and secularized it for a contemporary, popular culture.

These films both commend or critique contemporary culture and traditional religion. *Waterworld* is an apocalyptic film based on contemporary dilemma. It takes the warnings of global warming. As a secular apocalypse, *Wateworld* reflects current secular concerns rather than sacred ones in its depiction of the apocalyptic disaster. *Twelve Monkeys* is about Terry Gilliam's convoluted story that jumps from future to past to past-future and back again. The film is set in Philadelphia in 2035. Ninety-nine per-cent of the world's population has been destroyed by a killer virus that was released in 1996. The survivors of the virus have retreated underground, to a subterranean hell beyond the city. They decide to launch a time-travelling mission to 1996 to locate the source of the virus so as to defeat the bug and once again populate the earth's surface. The scientists believe a group called the *Army of 12 monkeys* was responsible for the outbreaks.

Finally, apocalypse is often used in the sense of a transition from this world, era, or state of being to another. Lewicki argues that true apocalyptic must maintain a tension between fear of this world and hope of deliverance in a new world, a contention echoed by Wilder's claim that apocalyptic must entail yea-saying to a new order and no-saying to the old one. [63] Hodder insists that the apocalyptic is essentially about "the passing of the old order and the creation of the new."[64] Lewicki stresses the start of a new, divine age.[65] He also argues that apocalypse is a form of discourse that makes use of the "universal cultural theme of cosmic destruction and universal renewal."[66]

Disagreements and lack of consensus should not be surprising for any term with such a wide usage and ancient pedigree. Apocalyptic as an analytic term lends an exotic, religious, even mystic tone to that to which it is applied. Moorhead correctly argues that apocalyptic is hard to define precisely because in its original religious context it "is but one thread in a complex theological tapestry, derived from the Bible."[67]

Different writers and speakers feature one facet or another from out of whose complexity so as to further the scholarly, religious or political purposes they have in mind. For instance, Ketterer[68] elevates the status of science fiction from drugstore pulp to serious literature by foundational apocalyptic's characteristics of an impending new world-a characteristic of science fiction as well and Kermode[69] promotes the novel insight to a theory of fiction by identifying the insight as the chief one entailed by a venerable and powerful discourse in Western thought, which is apocalyptic. The important thing is not to insist on one right usage for a complex term, but to explain the meanings and significance of the usage that one has in mind, a usage that intersects with one's subject.

A glance at the dominant modes of literary writing in the beginning of the 20 century reveals that an all-pervading sense of loss, doom, destruction etc shaped the literary expression of the major writers of the century, It has also been a century of wars-wars within and wars without and impending sense of doom loomed large always in its horizons. In fact, what is characterized as modernism in art and literature may well be seen as a manifestation of this mood. It could be argued that apocalypse has influenced almost all great novelists of the 20 century. Joyce's declaration in *Ulysses* that he wants to awaken from the nightmare of history, Conrad's cry of The horror, the horror' in *Heart of Darkness,* Lawrence's and Woolf s overwhelming sense of alienation of man occurring in their novels in general etc, all spring from the same mood. This century has also approximated in many respects the apocalyptic view of history and fate. Bruised hearts, disturbing minds, struggling and suffering masses, crisis of traditional values and breakdown of traditional narratives, tortured/hellish landscape of imagination, conflict and chaos at existential, religious, ethical and political plane. All these factors describe the apocalyptic history at its worst. Greene depicts these deserts of spirit desperate for April showers of faith and love. Greene's Catholic imagination is apocalyptic imagination by definition as Catholicism posits a fallen man, fragmented man in need of redemption, of fulfillment. This study argues that Greene is an apocalyptic writer in all the important senses in which the term has been used. His apocalyptic imagination finds expression in almost all his major works. *The Bible* depicts apocalyptic time as one of the approach of doom. This period is characterized by reversal of traditional hierarchies, confusion and confounding of values, evil disguises itself as good, and, in short, Satan's dominion is everywhere.

References

1. J.J. Collins. In Craig A. Evans & Stanly Porter (eds). *Apocalypse Literature: Dictionary of Newter. Backgrounds.* Downers Grove II., Intervarsity Press, 2004, p. 41.
2. See *The Revelation.* Chapter 5, 6-20 & 22.
3. Harold Rosenbarg. *The Tradition of the New.* New York: Horizon Press, 1959, p. 3.
4. Malcolm Bradbury in *A Dictionary of Modern Critical Terms,* ed. Roger Fowler. Routledge & Kegan Paul, 1987, p. 44.
5. Oswald Spengler. *Decline of the West.* Michigan: Farmington Hills. 1981.
6. Frank Kermode. *The Sense of an Ending. London*: Oxford Univ. Press, 1970, p. 23.
7. George Watson. 'The Empire of Lionel Trilling, '*Sewanee Review.* The John Hopkins University Press, 1927, p. 486.
8. *The Sense of an Ending,* p. 20.
9. Karl Marx's re-interpretation of history in terms of class

struggle as presented in the works like *The Communist Manifesto and Das Kapital,* Charles Dar - win's Theory of Evolution as presented in *The Origin of Species* and Sigmund Freud's ideas about human psyche and personally were undoubtedly the most cataclysmic in their influence upon the general western thought.

10. W,B. Yeats. "The Second Coming". *Michael Robartes and the Dancer.* Dublin: Cuala Press, 1919.
11. William Golding. *Lord of the Flies.* London: Faber and Faber, 1954.
12. R.W.B. Lewis. *Days of Wrath & laughter: Trials of the Word.* New Haven: Yale University Press, 1966, pp. 184-235.
13. John R. May. Toward a New Earth: *Apocalypse in the American Novel.* Notre Dame, Indiana: University of Notre Dame Press, 1972, p. 19.
14. *Towards a New Earth: Apocalypse in the American Novel,* p. 34.
15. David Ketterer: *New Worlds for Old:* Bloomington and London: Indian University Press, 1974. Pp. 3-14.
16. *New Worlds for Old,* p. 14-15.
17. Mary Shelley, *Frankenstein.* Lackington: Hughes, Harding, Mavor & Jones, 1818.
18. Mary Shellley. *The Last Man.* Lackington: Hughes, Harding, Mavor & Jones, 1826.
19. *New Worlds for Old,* p. 17
20. *New worlds for Old,* p. 16.
21. Veronica Hellinger. *Future/Present: The End of Science Fiction.* Berlin: Ulrich Ammon, 1996, p.22.
22. Paul Brains. *Nuclear Holocausts: Atomic War in Fiction* Kent, OH: Kant State University Press, 1987, pp 10-15.
23. *The Sense of an Ending,* p. 8-19.
24. John Kenneth Galbraith. *The Anatomy of Power.* Boston: Houghton Mifflin Co, 1983, p. 53.
25. Northop Frye. *Anatony of Criticism.* Princeton: Princeton University Press, 1957.
26. Bernard Bergonzie. *Situation of the Novel.* Hermonsds worth: Penguin Books, 1972, p. 175.

27. R. Buckminster Fuller. *Utopia or Oblivion: The Prospects for Humanity.* New York: Bantam Books Inc, 1972, p. 154.

28. Michael Barkun. *Disaster & the Millenium.* New Haven: Yale University Press, 1974, p. 204.

29. Eric Fromm. "The Present Human Condition: *Modern Essays.* Ed. Russel Nye. Illinois. Scott. Foresman and Company, 1963, p. 475.

30. Richard A. Falk. *This Endangered Planet.* New York: Viatage Books, 1972 p. 4.

31. John Maddox. *The Dooms Day Syndrome.* New York: Mc Gram Hill Book Company, 1972, pp. 3-144.

32. Robert Alter. 'The Apocalyptic temper.' In *Commentary* June, 1966, pp. 61- 62.

33. Ibid., pp. 61-66.

34. Kenneth L. Woodward, Angus deming, and Judith Gingold. "Apocalypse Chic." Newsweek. 17 Feb, 1975.

35. Ibid.

36. B. Magee. 'Getting Along Without Doomsday.' *Horizon:* 17. Summer 1975, p. 37.

37. Allan Ginsberg. "Playboy interview: Candid Conversation." *Playboy.* 16,4. April 1989, p. 242.

38. George Turner. *Down There in Darkness.* New York: Doherty Associates, 2000, p. 45.

39. Richard Dellamora. *Post modern Apocalypse. Theory and Cultural Practice at the End.* Philadelphia: University of Pennsylvania Press, 1995, p.111.

40. Richard Tarnas. *The Passion of the Western Mind: Understanding the Ideas that have Shaped our World Vied.* New York: Bellantine, 1991. P. 98.

41. Tarnas, 1991, p: 401.

42. Tarnas, 1991, p: 401.

43. Tarnas, 1991, p: 409.

44. Michael Barkum. *Disaster and the Millennium.* New Haven: Yale University Press, 1974, p. 18.

45. Michael Barkum. *Crucible of the Millennium: The Burned Over District of New York Syracuse: Syracuse university Press, 1986,* p. 153.

46. Barkum, 1986, p. 154.
47. Barkum, 1986, p. 155.
48. Barkum, 1986, p. 17.
49. Barkum, 1986, p. 17.
50. Barkum, 1986, p. 52.
51. Robert W. Brockway. *Myth from the Ice Age to Mickey Mouse.* Albang State University of New York Press, 1937, p. 79.
52. Brockway, 1937, p. 93.
53. Brockway, 1937, p. 93.
54. Brockway, 1937, p. 75.
55. Brockway, 1937, p. 80.
56. Brockway, 1937, p. 53.
57. Whitsun and Brewer. *Nearing the End. Urbana:* University of Illinois Press, 1989, p.11.
58. J.G. Melton. Cults, *Religion and Violence. New York*: Cambridge University Press, 2002, p 1.
59. John Whalen-Bridge. *The Apocalypric Complex – Origins, Histories.* Urbana: University of Illinois Press, 2001, p.37.
60. Robert Scheer. *Why We Don't Know Our Enemy.* Online: TruthDig. Com, 2006.
61. Why we Don't Know Our Enemy, 2006.
62. *Why we Don't Know Our Enemy, 2006.*
63. Amos N. Wilder. "Millennium and Utopia. A Study in the Background of the Idea of Progress" *The Journal of Religion,* 30, 4: 282-283. Oct., 1950.
64. A.D Hodder. "Emerson's Rhetoric of Revelation: Nature, the Reader, and the Apocalypse Within" *Journal of American Academy of Religion.* Pennsylvania State University Press. 1989, Vol. 60, No.4, pp. 786-788.
65. Zbigniew Lewqicki. *The Bang and the Whimper: Apocalypse and Entropy in American Literature.* Westport: Greenwood Press, 1984, p.37.
66. Lewqicki, 1984, p.52.
67. Lewqicki, 1984, p.23.
68. Lewqicki, 1974.
69. Lewqicki, 1970.

2

Graham Greene and the Passages to Epiphany

Graham Greene continues to fascinate critics and general readers alike and the reasons for this fascination are as much thematic as they are stylistic. Not only are Greene's novels fascinatingly readable but also have a striking appeal to the readers who find in them various portrayals of the condition of the modern man. Greene's career as a novelist reveals his perennial obsession with apocalyptic themes and ideas discussed in the last chapter. The genesis of this obsession lies in his childhood. The noisy and artificially moral atmosphere of the school bored him all the more. He likened the school to hell. In order to escape all the boredom and despair, Greene thought of putting an end to his life, or at least facing the risk of death. By chance, he found a revolver belonging to his brother with which he played the dangerous game of Russian roulette. He would put one bullet in the revolver, rotate the cylinder, place the muzzle of the revolver in his right ear and press the trigger, not knowing whether it would fall on the loaded chamber and bring about his death. This, he records in a collection of poems entitled *Babbling April,* the chief interest of which lies in a poem he called *The Gamble.* The following lines from the poem provide apt testimony to Greene's state of mind.

Place the revolver to my head
 And pull the trigger
Will it be mist and death.[1]

It becomes clear with the publication of Greene's recent novels and his two autobiographical works, *A Sort of Life* and *Ways of Escape,* that there is an important line of development leading from these earlier eschatological works to the more recent, highly secular ones. Greene's first eight novels, the most successful of which were *The Man Within*[2] and *Stamboul Train* [3] explored the divided loyalties between the public and private realms of life. The balance of loyalty between the public and private realms of life is a key theme throughout Greene's novels. His anxiety whether to be loyal to his father, the headmaster, or to his classmates caused him such stress that he underwent psychoanalysis when he was 16. It was also his experience with a class bully named Carter that helped form his awareness of evil and the consequence of betrayal in human interactions, all of which later shaped his works of fiction. In one of Graham Greene's novels, *The Comedians,* a character called Brown reflects:

> For the writers it is always said that the first twenty years of life contain the whole experience-the rest is observation, but I think it is equally true of all of us.[4]

Graham Greene's account of his childhood and adolescence reveals that the recurrence of seedy and obsessed backgrounds and extreme situations in his novels is an evidence of obsessional motifs in a single pattern in his early years. The past of a writer is of great value to him in novel-writing. Miriam Allot has said:

> Even if he withdraws from the world and shuts his eyes and stops his ears, his most distant past will begin to ferment. His childhood and youth alone are enough to provide a born novelist with an immense amount of literary nourishment. Nobody can stop the flow of the river which flows from him.[5]

Greene's novels and entertainments establish the truth of his statement. It is because so much of the experience communicated in his novels flows from Greene's memories that it is possible to view comprehensively in his works both the man who suffers and the mind which creates. Greene's unhappy childhood has had a seminal influence on all his fiction.

The guiding vision of the novelist is perceived by him once and for all early in his youth. The first dream which haunted him was about something outside that has got to come in. He also saw a man with his throat cut dragging himself across the carpet to the bed. These shocking dreams made the young Greene perceive evil as something frightfully real. But it was his later experience of public school which convinced him of the reality of hell. There, he remembers, he became aware of fear and hate, a kind of lawlessness – appalling cruelties. The conviction of hell on earth was re-inforced by his childhood reading. At first the works of Rider Haggard haunted him profoundly. In fact, Haggard's[6] exploration of the ordeal of entrapment influenced his imagination permanently. But later, when he was fourteen years old, Greene read a novel which determined his future. From the moment he picked up Marjorie Bowen's *The Viper of Milan,* he wanted to become a writer as he remembers it in *The Lost Childhood:*

> All the other possible futures slid a way... Imitation after imitation of Miss Bowen's magnificent novel went into exercise-books...It was as if he had been supplied once and for all with a subject.[7]

According to Greene, Miss Bowen's novel also provided him with a creative pattern,

> Perfect evil walking the world where perfect good can never walk again and only the pendulum ensures that after all in the end justice is done. [8]

He once told Philip Toynbee in an interview held at his residence:

> I write novels about what interests me, and I cannot write about anything else. And one of the things that interests me most is discovering the humanity in the apparently inhuman character.[9]

In addition to the childhood and youthful perceptions we may relate Greene's obsession with the sordid and violent aspects of life which the majority of his works have made us so familiar. Greene sees squalor and violence as the essence of human condition and from time to time he has sought them in the primitive sources of man's existence. He was, like Rimbaud and Conrad, fascinated by the dirt, the disease, the barbarity and the familiarity of Africa. The motive behind his Liberian trek was to get closer to a state of life, primitive and inchoate, where the manifestations of evil were undisguised. Like the bush devils, the squalor and brutality of the Liberian jungles enabled him to link up his personal childhood with the racial childhood of man. He records objectively all that he encountered – filth, disease, brutality, hardship and squalid discomfort. Africa explained to him the deep appeal of the seedy. It is nearer the beginning. He writes:

> There seemed to be a seediness about the place you couldn't get to the same extent elsewhere, and seediness has a very deep appeal: even the seediness of civilization, of the sky signs in Leicester Square, the tarts in Bond Street, the smell of cooking greens off Tottenham Court Road...It seemed to satisfy, temporarily, the sense of nostalgia for something lost; it seems to represent a stage further back.[10]

This is the atmosphere of Greene's novels and his characters, seedy in their failure and in the squalor of their lives, dwell not far from the central darkness. Violence and cruelty which, along with seediness, make up the milieu in which Greene's characters live. Greene writes:

> Today our world seems peculiarly susceptible lo brutality. There is a touch of nostalgia in the pleasure we take in the gangster novels, in characters who

> have so agreeably simplified their emotions that they have begun living again at a level below the cerebral. We, like Wordsworth, are living after a war and a revolution, and these hall- castes fighting with bombs between the cliffs of skyscrapers seem more likely than we to be aware of Proteus rising from the sea. It is not, of course, that one wishes to stay for ever at that level, but when one sees to what unhappiness, to what peril of extinction centuries of cerebration have brought us, one sometimes has a curiosity to discover if one can from what we have come, to recall at which point we went astray. [11]

In an article *The Lost Childhood,* [12] Greene remarks:

> When -perhaps I was fourteen at the time- I took Miss Marjorie Bowen's *The Viper of Milan* from the library shelf, the future for better or worse really struck. From that moment I began to write... Why? On the surface *The Viper of Milan* is only the story of a war between Gian Galezaao Visconti, Duke of Milan, and Mastino Delia Scala, duke of Verona, told with zest and cunning and an amazing pictorial sense. Why did it creep and color and explain the terrible living world of the stone stairs and the never quiet dormitory?...As for Visconti, with his beauty, his patience and his genius for evil, I had watched him pass by many a time in his black Sunday suit smelling of mothballs. His name was Carter. He exercised terror from a distance like a snowcloud over the young field. Goodness has only once found a perfect incarnation in a human body and never will again, but evil can always find a home there. Human nature is not black and white but black and Grey.[13]

Loyalty and betrayal were never a clear-cut thing for Greene. It could be subverted and its opposite could become a virtue, for no side was always right. It was this sense of the psychological divided mind and the clouded sympathies within the political and sexual realms that characterized the dark plots and anguished, alienated characters of his novels.

Greene is a man with a commitment to a religious tradition which he cannot see manifested in contemporary society: there is no apparent way of expressing belief with these physical, human materials—one can only express the absence of belief. Perhaps the best expression of this sense of the world is in the long passage from Newman[14] which stands as an epigraph to his Mexican travel book, *The Lawless Roads (U S title: Another Mexico).* In it Newman describes the fearful, suffering condition of men. It sets the tone and defines the world of Greene's imagination so well that it is worth quoting in full:

> To consider the world in its length and breadth, its various history, the many races of man, their starts, their fortunes, their mutual alienation, their conflicts; and then their ways, habits, governments, forms of worship; their enterprises, their aimless courses, their random achievements and acquirements, the impotent conclusion of long-standing facts, the tokens, so faint and broken, of a super-intending design, the blind evolution of what turn out to be great powers or truths, the progress of things, as if from unreasoning elements, not towards final causes, the greatness and littleness of man, his far-reaching aims, his short duration, the curtain hung over his futurity, the disappointments of life, the defeat of good, the success of evil, physical pain, mental anguish, the prevalence and intensity of sin, the pervading idolatries, the corruptions, the dreary hopeless irreligion, that condition of the whole race, so fearfully yet exactly described in the Apostle's words, "having no hope, and without God in the world"—all this is a vision to dizzy and appal; and inflicts upon the mind the sense of a profound mystery, which is absolutely beyond human isolation.

What shall be said to his heart-piercing, reason-bewildering fact? I can only answer, that either there is no Creator, or this living society of men is in a true sense discarded from His presence... if there be a God, since there is a God, the human race is implicated in some terrible aboriginal calamity. Newman was describing sinful, fallen man in terms of Christian doctrine, but his vision of humankind—fearful, defeated, and alone—might just as well be described in the contemporary language of alienation and anxiety. And the same is true of Greene's characters; they may be lapsed Catholics, or whisky priests, but their situations are metaphors for the human condition and in this sense Greene's novels are relentlessly contemporary.[15]

One might say that in Greene's novels calamity goes on, a continuing evidence that men have been discarded from God's sight. Hence, not only the seedy texture of the novels and the insistent violence, but also the tone of horror and disgust, a tone which sometimes seems to be in excess of the circumstances-for the most important fact about Greene's world is that God has abandoned it, and that fact cannot be represented as a part of the world, but only as an emotion about it. There is, therefore, a correlation between the banality and ugliness of this world and the spiritual emptiness of it, and this correlation is most powerful and emotionally affective. Greene's own theories of the shaping of his mind confirm this reading of his work, for he has always stressed the formative influences of early experience, and the continuity of consciousness. One form of this theory is what Greene calls the "Judas Complex"—the idea that the cruelties and betrayals of adult lives are born in childhood that guilts are rooted in innocence. The theory appears in Greene's autobiographical essay, *The Lost Childhood,* where it is epitomized in a quotation from a poem *Germinal* by George Russell, "In the lost boyhood of Judas Christ was betrayed".[16] For Greene evil is inseparable from man and from the world that man inhabits. It is significant to note that his Catholic persuasions convinced him of a metaphysical presence of evil. In his novels he is primarily preoccupied with this kind of evil, which then manifests itself in concrete terms most poignantly in the modem age of war, depression and social disintegration. For Greene, Catholic Christianity offers the only acceptable explanation for the overwhelming predominance of evil in the world. Criticizing Dickens he notes: "Evil appears only as an economic factor, nothing more. Christianity is a woman serving soup to the poor."[17] Greene's artistic imagination bears a strong imprint of Newman's idea of the world as implicated in some aboriginal calamity. The sense of this aboriginal calamity, the impending doom of the civilization, and the crisis of the age exercised such an influence on Greene that his whole outlook of the world and life also underwent a change which could be felt in his comments on life as:

> A life is, after all, a pretty chaotic affair—and I'm not thinking just of my own life but of the one which goes on around us. During the First World War I was old enough to realize what was happening. My father was always reading the paper to find out how many of his Old Boys had been killed in the course of the week. Then we lived through the Second World War, and I think we were all strongly impressed with the sense of chaos. After that revolutions, guerrilla warfare...disorder rather than an evil fate. Upheavals in South America, coups *d'etat,* terrorism. We are part of the world, aren't we? We're affected by this sort of life. We are at the heart of disorder.[18]

Greene wrote in his autobiographies and his personal diary that he seriously believed that the end of the world was approaching as prophesied in *The Bible* and this was what linked him to the tradition of apocalypse. Beliefs and narratives about the end of the world have fascinated people throughout human history. In nearly every society, sacred narratives are told about worldly cataclysm, the regeneration of the earth, and the creation of a terrestrial paradise. Until recently, the end of the world was interpreted as a meaningful, transformative and supernatural event involving the annihilation and renewal of the earth by deities or divine forces. During the last half of the twentieth century the creation and proliferation of nuclear weapons, in particular, have fundamentally altered contemporary thought, fueling fears of global annihilation and evoking widespread fatalism about the future of humanity. The dropping of atomic bombs on Hiroshima and Nagasaki in August 1945 initiated an era of nuclear apocalypticism that has flourished in American religious and secular cultures. Despite the end of the Cold War, anxieties about the possibility of nuclear apocalypse persist today, stemming from the magnitude and seeming uncontrollability of nuclear weapons and the likelihood that they will be developed and used by hostile nation or extremist organizations in the future. In addition to the fear of nuclear annihilation, other threats have emerged as possible causes or signs of impending doom and have enkindled apocalyptic speculation. Perhaps, T.S. Eliot was right when he said in one of his poems that the world ends not with a bang but with a whimper-the gradual destruction of the environment, the greenhouse effect, ozone depletion, the AIDS epidemic, widespread famine, overpopulation, incurable strains of pneumonia, Ebola, and flesh eating viruses.[19]

The twentieth century writers expressed the anxiety and uncertainty caused by the wars in different ways. Graham Greene is one such writer on whom the two World Wars exercised such an influence that it shaped his career as a novelist. He expressed his apocalyptic vision not only in his war novels in which he highlights the destruction caused by the wars but also in his religious novels in which he deals with seedy settings, squalor, dehumanization, moral and spiritual degradation which are the different secular manifestations of apocalypse. Greene had made the following observations on war which validate the claim that war had gone very deep in his psyche: "War is very like a bad dream in which familiar people appear in terrible and unlikely disguises." [20] And:

> When a war ends one forgets how much older oneself and the world have become: It needs something like a piece of furniture or a man's hut to awaken the sense of time.[21]

The year 1937 saw the outbreak of the Civil War in Spain. This war was caused by the uprising of the right-wing union of parties under General Franco against the Republican Government having communist leanings. Both the sides received support from abroad. Whereas the Socialists and the Communists all over the world supported the Republican government, General Franco's forces received support from Mussolini, Hitler and the Roman Catholic Church of Vietnam. This horrible bloody war ended in the victory of General Franco in 1939. As E H Carter and R A F Mears remark, it also crystallized opinion in every country. Britain and France being divided in opinion and unable to risk a fight, maintained precarious neutrality and were abused by Fascists and Communists alike. Being a Catholic, Greene must have felt like supporting General Franco's forces fighting against the anti-clerical Republican government, but his humanistic ardour must have impelled him to favour the communism-inclined government. Thus, he was in a strange predicament and his loyalties were divided. This predicament is reflected in his entertainment *The Confidential Agent*[22] wherein he is found sympathizing with both the sides represented by the agents D. and L. who approach various countries including Britain for aid and for supply of material to their sides.

Another great event that has had influence on Greene's novels is the World War II (1939-44). The years preceding the War were times of great tension, and there was an all pervading fear of an impending disaster. In London, telephones were cut off, anti-aircraft guns set up on Clapham Common and trenches were being dug. Air raid wardens had been appointed and air-raid posts set up in anticipation of war and the inevitable onslaught of German bombers. Greene believed that under the conditions of war novels, short stories, reviews and articles would not be saleable products, and the subsequent loss of earnings would make it difficult to support his family. By 14 September 1938, war seemed inevitable and Greene wrote in his diary:

> A curious air of unreality a rather silent [Clapham] Common—too many strangers talking together in pairs. The papers: CRISIS LATEST, FRENCH WAR CHIEFS HERE, HITLER CALLS HIS GENERALS, THE NEXT FEW HOURS WILL DECIDE PEACE OR WAR.' In the context of impending war Graham, the least domesticated of men, found some peace in domesticity. This is how he records his sense of impending doom: 'Nothing to do but go out and look at the latest posters. This heavy day, one feels, can't end in peace.[23]

September was filled with fear and uncertainty. On 14 September, the Prime Minister, Neville Chamberlain, flew to Berchtesgaden to meet Hitler as tension grew in France and Britian. On 22 September, Chamberlain returned to Germany and met the German leader again at Dodesberg. Two days later, Greene wrote in his diary:

> Chamberlain's second meeting with Hitler apparently ended in failure...Back again where we were on September 14 with war almost certain.. .a dreadful unreality over everything.[24]

When Hitler renounced all belligerent intentions against Britain, there was a great sense of relief in Britian—many felt that Chamberlain had saved civilization. Three months' respite from the fear of impending war followed. At last the message percolated through to Britain that Hitler's desire for domination was insatiable. As war seemed inevitable, Greene posted off to Huebsch the suggestion that he might write a blow-by-blow account of life in bombed London:

> It has occurred to me that in the event of this silly war was coming off, you might be interested in a book called something like THE FIRST HUNDRED DAYS which would be a personal account of conditions in a bombed London—what is happening in newspaper offices, suburban homes, accounts of raids, rumours, gossip, all the things that newspapers leave out because they don't consider them important. It will be a very queer city indeed, down to Victorian size in population. An empty Piccadilly, what a dread! I think a fascinating and bizarre piece of reportage could be done.[25]

The final act leading to war was German's invasion of Poland on 1 September 1939. Chamberlain issued an ultimatum that unless German forces withdrew from Poland, a state of war would exist. There was no response from Germany and on Sunday, 3 September, war was declared: "Everything that I have believed in during my public life has crashed in ruins,"[26] Chamberlain said movingly. He at last recognized that the country would be fighting "evil things, brute force, bad faith, injustice, oppression and persecution."[27] On seeing his first bombed house, one in Woburn Square neatly sliced in half, Greene recalled his sense of shock:

> With its sideways exposure it looked like a Swiss chalet: there were a pair of skiing sticks hanging in the attic, and in another room a grand piano cocked one leg over the abyss...In the bathroom the geyser looked odd and twisted seen from the wrong side, and kitchen impossibly crowded with furniture until one realized one had been given a kind of mouse-eye view from behind the stove and the dresser...[28]

Few writers have provoked such contradictory assessments during their life time as Graham Greene. A broad sweep of literary ancestors have been summoned up to explain the idiosyncrasies of his style and thought, from those acknowledged by Greene himself, such as Conrad, James Joyce , Dostoevsky, Kafka, the nineteenth century Decadents and the French Existentialists. This mesh of literary cross-judgments has been woven out of Greene's peculiar contradictory development, for he is Catholic convert whose books and particularly his religious novels have earned him an international reputation rare among contemporary English writers. Greene's first novel announces in its opening paragraph the arrival of a new voice in English fiction which is like this:

> He came over the top of the down as the last light failed and could almost have cried with relief at the sight of the wood below. He longed to fling himself down on the short stubbly grass and stare at it, the dark comforting shadow which he had hardly hoped to see. Thus only could he cure the stitch in his side, which grew with each jolt, jolt of the stumble downhill. The absence of the cold wind from the sea that had buffeted him for the last half hour seemed like a puff of warm air on his face, as he dropped below the sky. As though the wood were a door swinging on a great hinge, a shadow moved up towards him and the grass under his feet changed from gold to green, to purple and last to a dull grey. Then night came.[29]

The above quote is simply the guarantee of a mind and artistic sensibility strong enough to have its own vision and modes of expression even from an early stage. Joseph Conrad's *Heart of Darkness*, which shows how far Europeans have forgotten or deceived themselves about the abomination which lies beneath the surface of civilization, is a story to be kept in mind when reading Greene. The recurrence of certain types of characters and their situations in his works leads one to sense the working of obsessions in Greene's mind. These obsessions constitute an inescapable challenge to his readers. There is his primary obsession with evil, the dark side of human nature and life, produced by his acute sensitivity to the varied experiences in childhood. Later, his radical experiences and observations of cruelty, violence and ugliness in lands as far as Liberia, Mexico, Indo-China and Haiti served as accretions to his childhood awareness. This obsession accounts for a number of recurrent themes and motifs which form a matrix of impulses and circumstances for Greene's characters. Isolation and failure, guilt and betrayal, squalor and corruption, crime and violence, sin and suffering, childhood traumas and adult perversions, all these symbolize or dramatize the evil which permeates Greene's world. Greene's preoccupation with evil is inextricably linked with his religious consciousness of which Catholicism constitutes an important part.

Greene described the imaginative role that Catholicism played in his long writing career by making the allusion cited below to his literary hero, Henry James. "There does exist a pattern in my carpet constituted by Catholicism, but one has to stand back in order to make it out."[30] Greene's cycle of novels stands as the golden standard of what is often referred to as the "Catholic novel" in English literature.[31] Greene's unorthodox treatment of orthodox ideas created ambiguities and made it difficult to definitively clarify his attitude. Because of this critical fixation with religious un/orthodoxy in so much criticism of Greene, he has been labelled at various times a Manichean, Jansenist, Palegian, Quietist and existentialist.[32] Though Greene denied all these labels, the extreme situations of his characters and plots lend weight to such accusations of heresy being imposed upon him and upon his characters. In truth, Greene's paradoxical literary expression of Catholic faith is never offered as a comforting way out of the discomforting realities of modernity. Rather, Catholicism serves to heighten the awareness of the fallen sense of the world and challenge characters to respond to extreme situations in full knowledge of what is at stake. Religion-Catholicism in particular-inevitably becomes part of Greene's dark and seedy terrain, an imaginative ground from which Greene's creativity draws inspiration. However, determining just how important that religious terrain is, and how much "catholic" it is, has been a source of contention throughout the development of Greene criticism:

> After the death of Henry James a disaster overtook the English novel....for with [his] death the religious sense was lost to the English novel, and with the religious sense went the sense of importance of the human act. It was as if the world of fiction had lost a dimension: the characters of such distinguished writers as Mrs. Virginia Woolf and Mr. E. M. Forster wandered like cardboard through a world that was paper thin. [33]

In countless literary articles and interviews of the 1930s, 1940s, and 1950s, Greene bemoaned the loss of the "religious sense" in the English novel, for him, that sense became intimately tied to Catholicism-a faith tradition that could still evoke a metaphysical understanding of good and evil in the world and within an individual. His articles on writers of the period highlight this point. In his *Collected Essays,*[34] Greene writes that Conrad:

> had retained of Catholicism (an) ironic sense of an omniscience and of the final unimportance of life under the watching eyes...in scattered phrases you get the memories of a creed working like poetry through the agnostic prose. [35]

It was not until the early nineteenth century that British literary and philosophical writers began to reflect critically on the relationship between literature and religious belief. It found its literary expression in such writers as Samuel Taylor Coleridge, William Wordsworth, George Eliot and Mathew Arnold, to name just a few. Their work describes the historical trajectory of literature in terms of a *Deus Absconditus* (the Absconding god) of religion ever become eclipsed by Enlightenment, rationalism, science and philosophical idealism. What is left of the "religious sense" in the nineteenth century literature is expressed in either the moral allegories of George Eliot and Charles Dickens or in the poetic-philosophical displacement of religious feeling in many of the English romantic poets. The impression that religion had lost its power within British culture gained force in the Victorian elegies that mourned the loss of meaning in bourgeois culture and the implicit loss of religious belief. Eliot's *The Waste Land,* published in 1922, became the leitmotif of the early twentieth century, expressing the disillusionment, confusion, and seeming chaos that afflicted the generation of artists still reeling from World War I. Some writers persisted in offering substitutions for the traditional role that religion played In literary creativity-H G Wells placed his faith in science and the machine, G B Shaw in an optimistic secular humanism: D H Lawrence in the primal instinct of a lost sexual vitality; W H Auden, C Day Lewis, and Stephen Spender in their flirtation with an English socialism that could counteract the negative effects of an impersonal modern state. Many intellectuals in the 1930s and 1940s turned to orthodox religious belief in the Anglican Church, most notably T S Eliot, C S Lewis, Dorothy Sayers and, later, Auden. Surprisingly, after World War I, organized religion had regained some cultural prestige, a fashionable alternative for many British intellectuals looking for a cultural edifice that could stand up against the chaos, violence and meaninglessness around them. Thus in the early part of the twentieth century, Christianity, along with its rivals Marxism and psychoanalysis, found a place at the cultural table of intellectual debate.

The Protestant perspectives of these English literary figures matched the philosophical and theological investigations of such influential Protestant thinkers as David Friedrich Strauss, Soren Kierkegaard, Paul Tillich, and Northop Frye. These authors, like their literary relations, began with an initial supposition-the world of

Western civilization was in religious decline. Much of the impetus of their writing was to "shore up the fragments" of religious thought against "the ruin" of modernity in order to accomplish the difficult task of correlating the importance of religion to human existence. This valuable critical heritage is still a dominant model today for studying the relationship of literature and religion, effectively placing theology at the service of explicating literature and assessing the concerns of literary criticism.[36]

If religion is to find a home in contemporary literature, the logic goes, it can no longer be understood in terms of orthodox systems of belief, religious markers or theological nomenclature. Religion must be reframed in existential or psychological terms so that literature has a religious value because, at its heart, it expresses ultimate concern, mystery or the infinite in human life. It assumes, in effect, that good literature, as a human artefact, has a latent, unconscious theological character that manifests itself in the uncertain, the tragic, or what Tillich called the *demonic*[37] aspect of contemporary life. Situated within any discussion of the religious dimension in literature is the rise of the "Catholic Novel" in the early twentieth century. The "Catholic novel" in Europe originated in the neo-romantic and decadent forms of French literature in the nineteenth and early twentieth centuries as a reaction against the dominant discourse of Enlightenment philosophy and the antireligious doctrines of the French Revolution.[38] Such writers as Joris- Karl Huysmans, Leon Bloy, Charles Peguy, Georges Bernanos, Francois Maurice and Paul Claudel made the catholic novel into an accomplished literary form that opposed positivist thought and defended the spiritual reality of human life in terms of a distinctly Catholic ontology and epistemology. These authors drew their poetic and thematic material from their common Catholic experience and beliefs, framing and structuring their artistic vision through the lens of Catholic dogma, symbolism and religious conversion.[39] Thus, the Church's sacramental life; its complex rituals, doctrines, and mystical tradition; and its emphasis on the primacy of theological aesthetics over rational modes of theological discourse served to address and critique the reigning ideology of bourgeois, materialist French society. Catholicism was both a reactionary critique of the state of religious decline in modernity and a powerful theological, philosophical and artistic alternative to this seeming decline. In terms of theme and plot, the French Catholic novel contained many classic ingredients. David Lodge, in the introduction to Francois Mauriac's *The Viper's Tangle*, succinctly describes these key attributes in the following manner:

> the idea of the sinner's 'being at the heart of Christianity' (Peguy's phrase), the idea of 'mystical substitution,' the implied criticism of materialism, (and) the tireless pursuit of the erring soul by God, the 'hound of Heaven' in Francis Thompson's famous metaphor. [40]

Another basic ingredient that heightened the tension of the genre's narrative and plot is the conflict between the corrupt flesh and the transcendent spirit, usually devised as sexual tension between male and female protagonists, ascending to a spiritual suffering that finds its reference in Christ's crucifixion. What is remarkable about these French Catholic authors who typify this genre is the accessibility of their writing to those who do not share a Catholic sensibility.

Paralleling the Catholic revival of France was the very different experience of English Catholicism, a minority tradition in predominantly Protestant England. It was not until the 1840s that Catholicism gained some legitimate status in England. Following from this legal victory and aided by John Henry Newman- a convert from Anglicanism's own religious revival, the Oxford Movement-a small but effective Catholic revival flourished in England for over one hundred years. From the beginning, it was dominated by English converts who shared a vision of the world as fallen, or in Newman's words, "implicated in some terrible aboriginal calamity."[41]

Although Greene disliked being called a Catholic yet he elaborated his debt to Newman's perspective in his conversations with Allain:

> My books only reflect faith or lack of faith, with every possible human in between. Cardinal Newman, whose books influenced me a great deal after my conversion, denied the existence of a 'Catholic' literature. He recognized only the possibility of a religious dimension superior to the literary dimension, and he wrote that books ought to deal first with what he called in the vocabulary of the day, the tragic destiny of man in his fallen state/ I agree with him. It is the 'human factor' that interests me, not apologetics.[42]

Greene was so much influenced by John Henry Newman that in the epigraph to his travel book on Mexico, *The Lawless Roads,*[43] Greene quotes from Newman's *Apologia Pro Vita Sua,* a text that documents the theologian's own gradual conversion to Catholicism:

> The defeat of good, the success of evil, physical pain, mental anguish, the prevalence and intensity of sin, the pervading idolatries, the corruptions, the dreary hopeless irreligion...inflicts upon the mind the sense of the profound mystery which is absolutely beyond the human situation...if there be a God, since there is a God, the human race is implicated in some terrible aboriginal calamity.[44]

This aboriginal calamity is the world of Greenland, a landscape filled with lonely, pathetic and sometimes malevolent characters. Incidents of pursuit, acts of violence and voluntary and involuntary betrayal populate a world set against a background of misery and squalor. Greene's characters live as exiles on the extreme edges of society, conscious of their failures and their betrayals of one another. Throughout his texts, the eschatological certainties of both Christianity and Marxist ideology are always thwarted by the inevitability of human failure. Failure, as Terry Eagleton claims, is the one legitimate form of victory in Greene's victory in his novels, suggesting that the doctrine of Incarnation finds its textual embodiment not so much in human creativity but in human failure—the tragic, radically fallen nature of humanity.[45]

Catholicism, thus, appeared more attractive to Greene than Anglicanism or Protestantism due to its recognition of the ultimate depravity of man, an idea that had been eclipsed in the latter due to excessive inclination towards individualism as an ultimate value. In fact Greene, along with Evelyn Waugh[46] are the two most notable figures to have pioneered the Catholic novel writing in England.

With the novels of Evelyn Waugh and Graham Greene, the Catholic genre found a popular preeminence in England in the 1930s and 1940s. Waugh's conversion was anchored in his belief that the essential truths of Catholicism had been dissipated by an English society uprooted from its Catholic birthright. His early satires humorously exposed modern society as a vacuous spectacle adrift from its roots. Beginning with the novel *Brideshead Revisited,* published in 1944, he attempted to use Catholicism not only to frame the issues and crisis of modern society but also to offer Catholicism's vision and doctrine as an antidote to the present crisis in Western, and specifically, English civilization. Waugh's later books, true to the author's own religious conversion to Catholicism, portrayed characters searching for certainty and triumph of a creedal faith that had been obscured or eclipsed by the mores and values of modern European society. Waugh's political and social conservatism fit nicely into Protestant category's of what an "English" expression of the Catholic novelist might look like.

Graham Greene, also a convert, shares with Waugh much of the same Catholic concerns and issues in his writing, but in many ways he comes closer than Waugh to dramatizing the themes of the Catholic novel as embodied by his French contemporaries. The classic ingredients elucidated by David Lodge concerning Francois Mauriac's Catholic vision-the sinner at the heart of Christianity, mystical substitution, a critique of materialism, and God as the Hound of Heaven-can be found in many of Greene's most celebrated works.

Greene's novels of the 1930s, 1940s and 1950s, like those of Waugh. Mauriac, and Bernanos, were constantly discussed in terms of how well or how ambiguous was the correlation of character and plot to the Catholic theological categories of scholastic thought. The dialectical nature of counter-Reformation Catholicism, attempting to stand against both Protestant religious discourse and the materialism and secular ideologies of the modern age, found its literary expression in these Catholic writers of the early part of the century. There has been a growing consensus by critics in the 1970s and 1980s that the Catholic novel as Genre, with its formulaic themes and theological certitudes, has disappeared as Roman Catholicism shed its opposition to serious engagement with the modern world.[1] Gene Kellogg notes that the genre:

> began when the isolation of the world's Roman Catholic communities started to break down in the nineteenth century, and which tapered off-perhaps ended- when Roman Catholics 'joined the modem world' after the Second Vatican Council.[48]

More derisively, Albert Sonnenfeld eulogizes the Catholic novel's demise by maintaining that

> Vatican II marked the legitimization and consecration of a host of modernist longings that were both a reflection and a cause of the 'decline and fall' of that possibly preserves and reactionary nostalgia which made the Catholic Novel possible.[49]

These critics interpret the net effect of the Second Vatican Council as the Church's assimilation into modernity, an intellectual appropriation of Catholicism to the philosophical and theological concerns of Enlightenment discourse. If Greene was an astute student of the Catholic literary revival of France and a major contributor to its success as a viable genre in England, labelling him in such a constructive manner proves difficult, for Greene's artistic concerns and his vision of reality transgressed the theological boundary, as well as the historical era, of the Catholic novel. As much as Greene's texts evade such a simple designation, there is a redundancy and uniformity in the criticism from this period, especially in terms of assessing Greene's position in the literary canon. Many Catholic critics of the time championed Greene's work for manifesting their faith in such a popular medium, even as they became obsessed about whether the author and his characters were Palegian, Manichean, or Gnostic heretics. Even those critics who concurred that Greene's religious themes are paramount in interpreting his novels argued that his creativity as a writer came from a very limited and biased point of view. David Pryce-Jones's 1963 study, which looks almost exclusively at the religious aspect of Greene's texts, reproaches his use of Catholicism as merely a clever tactic on the author's part to superimpose paradoxical situations into his melodramas.[50] Still others of the period lamented that so much attention had been given to the Catholic dimension in these novels. John Atkins complains in his 1957 comprehensive study that the constant attention paid to Catholicism and theology obscures the more important literary theme and issues, noting that:

> Greene's work is valuable as social commentary and much more as individual (including personal revelation...the theology is on the surface) planted there rather weightily but it is a surface growth.[51]

Thus, from the beginning Greene criticism has been polarized by what one makes of the religious sense, a quality that Greene claimed was of utmost importance to the modem novel. The argument continued even after

Greene rejected the formal elements of the Catholic novel genre in his works following his famous Catholic cycle. Consequently, the critical community-those both sympathetic and unsympathetic to a religious reading of the novel by and large- assign to his most famous works the rubric of the Catholic novel, whereas his later works are often classified in political and psychological terms because secular concerns seem to predominate in his themes and plots. As the Second Vatican Council began to give privilege to and accentuate new paradigms in the Catholic Church's self-understanding and in its relationship to the modern world, so too there is a material transformation of the religious imagination of writers engaged in that faith tradition. Graham Greene is one such a writer who profits from broadening the vantage point, for he illustrates the problems and the preoccupations that have formed both the consciousness and the religious imagination of the twentieth century.

With the success of *Brighton Rock,* Greene entered into his most productive years of writing, producing a series of novels that explored the boundaries and loyalties of religious faith as understood in the confines of the Catholic consciousness of his characters. The themes in Greene's early novels, beset with criminals and conspirators, alienated protagonists and betrayal of loyalties, actually find expression in all his great novels of this middle period: the Catholic Pinkie in *Brighton Rock,* who conspires to marry Rose in the fallout of a gang murder; the whisky priest in *The Power and the Glory,* who betrays his celibate vows by fathering a child; the convert Scobie in *The Heart of the Matter,* whose double loyalties to wife and mistress cause his suicide; and the adultery of Bendrix in *The End of the Affair,* who plays a game of loyalty and betrayal among his mistress, her husband and her God. In each case, Greene's use of Catholicism extends the psychological and moral crisis of characters beyond their own deception and treachery and places it in confrontation with the objective reality of God. In the end, Greene illustrated that one's faith and belief in God is as treacherous a place as that of the world of politics and espionage.

Robert Pendleton[52] argues that Greene's Catholic novels were only a psychological and stylistic detour from his "Conradian Masterplot," perhaps an unconscious attempt by Greene to create a genre that set him apart from the overt homage his thrillers owed to Conrad's narrative themes and protagonists. Building on Harold Bloom's well-known study, *The Anxiety of Influence.*[53] Pendleton suggests that Greene's Catholic novels operate as "deviations" and "displaced repetitions" of Conrad's interiorized thrillers. Greene's later novels, he argues, return to the larger influence of Conrad, where faith and belief are so marked by skepticism that they signify the loss of religious meaning for his characters.[54] And Cates Balbridge, in an otherwise nuanced discussion of the conception of God in Greene's novels, uses J. Hillis Miller's *The Disappearance of God: Five Nineteenth Century Writers* [55] to argue that Greene's obsession with divided loyalty illustrates the author's psychological and spiritual quest for "a consummation or a reconciliation or a reintegration that he can never quite—or at best only fleetingly-realize."[56]

Balbridge concludes that Greene, like William Blake, created his own peculiar and powerful religious system that, seen over the span of his novels, divested itself of any orthodox form of Catholicism; rather, he argues that Greene's deity is imagined as one in the midst of cosmic entropy, emphasizing a God who is only worthy of the pity of failure, never a God who might triumph in the world, much less in the human person. What is interesting about both Pendleton and Balbridge's argument is how it returns to the Protestant English tradition that stresses in literature the absence of God, or at least God's virtual impotence and demise in the modem world. Greene's works can be divided into Catholic and Post-Catholic works and they are shaped by the developments in Roman Catholicism that resulted from the Second Vatican Council. Catholic theology before Vatican II was primarily a hermetic, scholastic endeavour that stressed the individual's status before God in terms of moral of moral precepts and ritual obligations.

Greene's artistic confrontation with his religious imagination parallels the developments in Catholic theology, doctrine, and liturgy since Vatican II. When Greene returns to explicitly religious themes in his late novels, he is not merely reworking the dialogue with the political concerns, as well as the religious crisis, of belief that have become part of the experience of Catholicism since the end of the Council.

Graham Greene marks a departure from other novelists of the twentieth century. Twentieth century literature is characterized by a revolt against all forms of dogma especially the Christian dogma that was inherited by the twentieth century novelists as a legacy. The eminent novelists of twentieth century like D H Lawrence, E M Forster, James Joyce and Woolf revolted against the traditional idea of religion parodying it in different forms. D H Lawrence parodied the Christian ethics in different novels. James Joyce parodied the concept of Hell in *A Portrait of the Artist as a Young Man* and also Christian ethics in *Ulysses.* Virginia Woolf parodied it in her agnosticism and E M Forster parodied it in his commitment to humanistic ideals like rationalism and democracy. On the other hand, Greene's outlook of modern man's crisis is a product of his apocalyptic vision which is derived from the Bible.

Although Greene does not foresee sudden events of catastrophe striking the world, but he is significantly attracted to the idea of man's regression running parallel to the alleged progression as a social animal. One of the characteristic features of Greene as an apocalyptic writer is that he envisions all the emancipatory projects, all social, political and economic narratives as ultimately contributing to a slow but sure catastrophe. Despite his Catholicism, Greene hardly suggests a final redemption of man as a social being but this does not contradict his catholic outlook since Catholicism and *The Bible* ultimately sees redemption and salvation only in spiritual terms. However, what, qualifies Greene as an apocalyptic writer is his interest in exploring how dehumanization manifests itself in worldly terms in various ways like corruption, lack of interest in life and love, evil disguised as good, establishing mini-narratives so as to substitute meta-narratives which have crumbled down but even these mini-narratives do not solace the characters of Greene perpetually. He moves from one substitute to another so as to fill the gap of the man within but still does not achieve salvation. Greene suggests that all enlightenment projects of emancipation miserably failed-an idea which is of central importance to post-modem apocalypse. Greene's significant ideas lie in his belief in the failure of human reason, all "isms", socialism, democracy, humanism, rationalism, empiricism and Marxism. All his novels have led a counter-revolution against the modernist tradition which dominated fiction during the early part of the century. As a result of all this, Greene has become the most eloquent voice of the anguished fears characterizing his time. His apocalyptic imagination is his appropriation of Catholic imagination and which can be characterized broadly in these terms. Separation of man from Divine Origin. Progressive degeneration. Increasing secularization in the unfolding of human history and the establishment of Mini-narratives.

References

1. Graham Greene. "The Gamble" in *Babbling April*. Oxford: Blackwell, 1952.
2. Graham Greene. *The Man Within*. London: Heinemann, 1929.
3. Graham Greene. *Stamboul Train*. London: Heinemann, 1932.
4. Graham Greene. *The Comedians*. London: Bodely Head, 1966, p. 23.
5. See Miriam Allot. *Novelists on the Novel. London:* Oxfoed Univesrity Press, 1957, p. 108.
6. Sir Henry Rider Haggard (1856-952) is best known for his

African adventure novels, notably *King Soloman's Mines* and *She.*

7. Graham Greene. *The Lost Childhood & Other Essays.* London: Barnes & Noble 1951, p. 23.
8. Greene, 1951, p. 25.
9. *The Hindustan Times,* September 19, 1957.
10. Graham Greene. *Journey without Maps.* London: Heinemann, 1936, pp. 7-8.
11. *Journey Without Maps,* p. 10.
12. Graham Greene. "The Lost Childhood" in *The Lost Childhood and Other Essays.* London: Eyre & Spottiswoode, 1951.
13. Greene, 1951, pp. 16-17.
14. John Henry Newman (1801-1890) began his career as an Anglican Churchman and scholar and ended it as a Roman Catholic cardinal.
15. Graham Greene. *The Lawless Roads.* London: Longman, 1939, p. 43.
16. Greene, 1951, p. 23.
17. Graham Greene. *Reflections.* London: Reinhardt, 1990, p. 0113.
18. Marie-Francoise Allian. *The Other Man: Conservations with Graham Greene.* London: Bodley Head, 1983, p. 16-17.
19. T.S. Eliot. "The Hollow Men." *Dial.* London: Rickard A. Parker, 1952.
20. Graham Greene. *The Ministry of Fear.* London: Heinemann, 1943, p.26.
21. Graham Greene. *The Tenth Man.* London: Bodely Head and Anthony Blond, 1985, p. 156.
22. Graham Greene. *The Confidential Agent.* London: Heinemann, 1939.
23. Graham Greene's *Diary.* 14 Sep. 1983.
24. *Ibid.*
25. Quoted in *Preface to Graham Greene.* London: Freedom Press, 1973.
26. Quoted in "The Tone of Disappointment", *The Daily Telegraph.* September 2, 1939.

27. Ibid.
28. Graham Greene. 'At Home'. *Collected Essays*. London: Bodley Head, 1981, p. 333.
29. *The Tenth Man,* pp. 2-3.
30. *The Other Man: Conservations with Graham Greene,* p. 159.
31. The designation of "Catholic" Novel as a genre and the distinction of being named as "Catholic" author applied to many authors like Evelyn Waugh and Mauriac, besides Greene, especially during the first half of the twentieth century.
32. A.A. De Vitis. *Graham Greene*. Boston: Twayne Publishers, 1986.
33. Graham Greene. *Collected Essays*. London: Penguin, 1969, p. 91.
34. Greene, 1969.
35. Greene, 1969. P. 140.
36. Robert Detweiler. *Breaking the fall: religious Readings of Contemporary Fiction*. San Francisco. Harper & Row, 1989, p.34.
37. Paul Tillich. *On Art and Architecture*. New York: Cross Road, 1987.
38. Theodore P. Fraser. *The Modern Catholic Novel in Europe*. New York: Macmillan, 1994, pp. 1-23.
39. Ellis Hanson. *Decadence and Catholicism*. Cambridge MA: Harvard University Press, 1997, p. 26.
40. David Lodge. *Introduction to Francois Mauriac: The Viper's Rangle*. New York: Carroll & Graf, 1987, p/xiv.
41. John Henry Newman. *Apologia pro Vita Sua*. London: J.M. Dent & Sons Ltd, 1864.
42. *The Other Man: Conservations with Graham Greene,* p. 150.
43. Graham Greene. *The Lawless Roads*. London: Longman, 1939.
44. Interview with V.S. Prichett for the *London Times,* 18 march 1978, p. 287.
45. Terry Eagleton. "Relucant heroes: The Novels of Graham Greene" in *Graham Greene: Modern Critical Views*. New York: Chelsea House, 1987, pp. 114-115.

46. Arthur Evelyn St. John Waugh (1903-1966). He had also converted to Catholicism like Greene and wrote Catholic novels like *Brideshead Revisited* and *Sword of Honour*.
47. Mary Gerhart and Anthony C. Yu. *"Morphologies of Faith"* Essays in religion and Culture. Atlanta GA: Scholars Press, 1990, p. 181-201.
48. Gene Kellogg. *The Vital Tradition: The catholic Novel in a Period of Convergence*. Chicago: Loyola University Press, 1970, p.4.
49. Albert Sonnefeld. *Crossroads: Essays on the catholic Novelists*. York SC: French Literature Publications, 1982, p.viii.
50. David Pryce-Jones. *Graham Greene*. London: Oliver & Boyd, 1963, 9. 100.
51. John Atkins. *Graham Greene*. London: Calder & Boyars, 1957, 1996, p. ix.
52. Robert Pendleton. *Graham Greene's Conradian Masterplot*. New York: St Martin's Press 1996, pp 5-7.
53. Harold Bloom. *Anxiety of Influence*. London: Oxford University Press, 1973.
54. Robert Pendleton, *Graham Greene's Conradian Masterplot*. New York: St. Martin's Press, 1996, p. 5-7.
55. J. Hillis Miller's *The Disappearance of God: Fove Nineteenth Century Writers* London: John Murray, 1952.
56. Cates Baldridge. *Graham Greene's Fictions: The Virtues of Extremity*. Columbia: University of Missouri Press, 2000, p. 4.

3

Dark Clouds and Graham Greene

Greene's literary imagination was deeply coloured by his preoccupation with evil which had found its most horrific expression in the destructive wars of the twentieth century, Greene evinces a sense of impending doom in some of the most impressive works including many novels written during this time. In fact, war and its effects on the European society form an important part of Greene's literary expression. In many novels that have been discussed in this chapter, Greene emerges as one of the most powerful voices predicting an all-encompassing catastrophe soon to overtake humanity. He thus shows signs of a movement towards a secular apocalypse that does not promise a regeneration or renewal after the final stroke of destruction.

Apocalyptic ideas traditionally have been associated with religious eschatologies, but secular apocalyptic culture has also contributed to widespread beliefs, images and expectations about the end of the world. Instead of faith in a redemptive new realm to be established after the present world is annihilated, secular doomsday visions are usually characterized by a sense of pessimism, absurdity, and nihilism. Secular apocalyptic ideas have become increasingly pervasive in contemporary society; these notions, however, are not unique to the twentieth century. Visions of the world destroyed by humans, as well as by natural cataclysms, began appearing in fictional literature in the 1800s. According to Warren Wagar[1] Mary Shelley's *The Last Man*[2] was the first of such works, and the majority of these early secular doomsday writings, like religious apocalyptic visions, offered the hope of a renewed and transformed society after the destruction of the world. Nineteenth century secular visions of worldly destruction and redemption of the working class as an explicit form of secularized millenarianism. As Eric Hobsbawm notes in his Primitive Rebels, the political ideals of socialism and communism resemble the millenarian "hope of a complete and radical change in the world."[3]

The nineteenth and early-twentieth-century visions of worldly destruction and transformation were usually optimistic in their evaluation of apocalypse, viewing it not as the end but the beginning of the transformation of society. Since the end of World War II, visions and beliefs about the end of the world appear to have become increasingly pessimistic, stressing cataclysmic disaster as much as previous millenarian visions emphasized the imminent arrival of a redemptive new era. Literary critics have made several assertions in their attempts to characterize the postmodern condition as an apocalyptic psychological and social milieu involving individual and collective perceptions of the decay and destruction of art, culture, philosophy and meaning:

> a *fin-de-millennium* consciousness which, existing at the end of history...uncovers a great arc of disintegration and decay against the background radiation of parody, kitsch, and burnout...a suicidal nihilism.. .on the violent edge between ecstasy and decay.[4]

Numerous scholars have suggested that the prophetic apocalyptic imaginings of the past have become secular apocalyptic realities in recent decades. As Daniel Wojcik[5] notes, Images of Hiroshima and Nagasaki, the Holocaust,

Vietnam (rendered by filmmaker Francis Ford Coppola as *Apocalypse Now*) give unalterable contours to the landscape of contemporary memory. As has already been discussed earlier that there are many books written by academics, scientists, and social critics which predicted the cataclysmic destruction or gradual decline of humanity as the result of human and natural causes. Since the development of nuclear weapons, a sense of profound anxiety and uncertainty has existed in all the societies about a future in which nuclear warfare is a possibility. The twentieth century writers expressed the anxiety and uncertainty due to the two World Wars in different ways. Graham Greene is one such writer on whom the two World Wars exercised such an influence that it shaped his career as a novelist. In addition to the two World Wars, his vision was further strengthened by the Spanish Civil War, the Vietnam War and the Cold Wars.

As discussed in the previous chapter, the two World Wars and other wars drastically affected Greene's outlook on the future of mankind, in general, and that of European man, in particular. It is during these years that Greene found a confirmation of his fears about the impending disaster that was likely to overtake the world. His whole literary sensibility became unalterably coloured by the experience of witnessing the unprecedented destruction and immeasurable suffering that followed it. Greene's Catholicism offered him little consolation in the face of such catastrophic series of events. In fact, his Catholicism takes on an unmistakable tinge of comprise with an alternate view that supposed that God had, at least during that period, abandoned mankind to suffer inconsolably. Greene's preoccupation with war related themes reveals how strongly he felt the sense of an ending that Kermode[6] describes as the most significant feature of the apocalypse. The wars created an omnipresent atmosphere of tension and fear and Greene's novels bear strong imprint of these events.

One of the very potent expressions of apocalypse, the

preoccupation with death, is a recurrent feature of Greene's novels especially the novels dealing with war most of which begin with or presume death and then circle back to that originating end as if time had stuck there and only a repetition of doom were possible. In his compulsion toward risk, both within and outside of his writing, Greene has endlessly pursued and forestalled death, appropriating what he calls the dangerous moment over and over again:

> I found myself tempting the end to come...I hadn't the courage for suicide, but it became a habit with me to visit troubled places, not to seek material for novels but to regain the sense of insecurity which I had enjoyed in the three blitzes on London.[7]

His eschatological obsession presents earthly reality retrospectively, as limbo or purgatory, where we are constrained to wander in search of an ending. In Greene's fallen world-where "goodness has only once found a perfect Incarnation in a human body and never will again"[8], evil alone partakes of transcendence. Four of Graham Greene's novels are set during the Second World War-*The Ministry of Fear (1943), The Heart of the Matter (1948), The End of the Affair (1951),* and *The Tenth Man (1985).* Only one was written and published during the war. The novel sets out to capture the specific timbre of wartime attitudes. Four short stories and a few essays written in wartime also capture the unmistakable aura of wartime life. *The Tenth Man*, published in 1985, was probably written in 1944 when Greene was under contact to MGM (Film makers).

The story of *The Tenth Man* by Graham Greene takes place in Paris and a French village in the 1940s during the German occupation of her in the Second World War. It starts off in a German prison with the narrator talking about the prisoners singling out two specific characters, the Mayor of Bourge, and Pierre, an engine driver. Through a situation concerning these two we are introduced to the main character, Jean-Louis Chavel, who changes his last name to Charlot. Chavel is one of a group of 30 Frenchmen who are held by the Germans as hostages to discourage resistance violence by the local people against them. However, the violence does take place and two Germans are killed. The German prison commander issues orders that one out of every ten hostages should be executed. The victims are to be chosen themselves by drawing lots. Chavel draws the last marked slip which condemns him to death and goes into hysteria. In his hysteria he offers to give everything he owned to someone if they died for him. A man named Janvier, thinking of his sister and mother, speaks up and takes his offer. After the agreement Janvier draws up a will leaving everything he now owned to his sister and mother. The next morning he is executed. After the liberation of France, Chavel is released from the prison and he meets Janvier's mother and sister. He finds shelter in the house and is employed there as a manservant. Gradually Chavel and Theresa begin to love each other. Meanwhile, an actor named Carosse comes there pretending to be Chavel and claiming his right over his Property. Chavel now reveals his identity. A duel follows between them in which both die.

The condition, of actual war suited Greene's own view of human condition; his fiction, particularly his early fiction, reflects both the anxious, doom-ridden mood of the era leading unto the Second World War itself and the ambiguous role of humans in that alienated and threatened world. And this depiction of the early writing is particularly accurate in so far as it relates to the basically Christian view of fallen man informing both the socio-political entertainments of the early period and the religious novels that began with *Brighton Rock* in 1938. Intrigue, treachery, double- dealing and warfare of one kind or another form the background to *A Gun For Sale (1936), Brighton Rock (1938),* and The *Confidential Agent (1939),* all written before the major European conflict broke out in 1939. An atmosphere of danger, decay and deadly opponents in a conflict that could resemble a schoolboy's game permeates Auden's poetry of the early thirties. What is Audenesque in verse of that decade involves the omnipresence of this very background of industrial decay, psychological unease, and testing of a kind associated with the public school ethos in character building and leadership.

Greene's penchant for the seedy and the stunted gives a personal stamp to his novels of the thirties, but their evocation of material decay matched by psychic ill health was typical of one of the prevailing literary moods of the period. Even Greene's style could be Audenesque at this point. His interest in the suppressed links between childhood experience and adult mental trauma, coupled with his gift for recreating a panorama of commonplace urban activity, produced a tone that can resemble Auden's. The passage in which Moggart makes the comment is so perceptive and so revealing of the texture of much writing in 1930s, which is worth quoting in full:

> The common qualities are pungent consciousness and a starting contract-a shock of surprise at the congruity of the relationship called up. This is usually produced by mating the abstract with the concrete, the idea or quality with the strikingly contemporaneous visual image. The effect can be sharp and stimulating; in addition, it can easily sound rather desperate and bitter. It is probably this quality which particularly attracted writers in this century. T.S.Eliot has streets "that fellow like a tedious argument".. .Graham Greene's *Ministry of Fear* begins: "There was something about a fair which...called him like innocence". In the thirties the smile was over-used and echoed from one poet to another, mainly under Auden's influence.[9]

The mood of impending disaster associated with slump, fascism triumphant and the slide into war during the thirties is easily recognizable. Its very recognizability has led many critics to comment on Greene's age of this mood in 1957. Morton Dauwen Zabel comments in this way on the opening scenes in *The Ministry of Fear.*

> Again we enter the familiar spectre of our age, years of fear and mounting Premonition in the 1930s, war and its disasters in the forties, its aftermath of treachery and anarchy still around as in the fifties: no matter what the decade. Greene's evocation of it through fourteen novels (of which *The Ministry of Fear* may be taken as typical of those he calls "entertainments") invariably brings with it an effect that he has made classic of its time.[10]

While such a statement can be usefully applied to the thirties, it is not an accurate comment on the forties, which involve wide fluctuations in mood. It is not even a helpful way of assessing Greene's writing about the war itself. The ethos in Britain varied, significantly during the war years, and Greene is an even better chronicler of these variations in mood than a commentator such as Zabel allows. To Zabel, *The Ministry of Fear* evokes an England typical of the century: "Here once more is the haunted England of the Twentieth Century, the European nightmare of corruption and doom". But how does one accommodate the following passage by Greene into such an atmosphere of corruption and doom?

> That, I think, is why one feels at home in London- or in Liverpool or Bristil, or any of the bombed cities- because life there is what it ought to be. If a cracked cup is put in boiling water it breaks, and an old dog toothed civilization is breaking now. The nightly routine of sirens, barrage, the probing raider, the unmistakable engine (where are you? Where are you? Where are you?") the bomb-bursts moving nearer and then moving away, hold one like a love-charm. We are not quite happy when we take a few days off.[12]

The date of this passage, October 1940, is close to the date of the opening scene in *The Ministry of Fear*. The description of the probing raider with its insistent question occurs in *The Ministry of Fear.* The exhilaration in Greene's essay here and in his Journal of the blitz, *The Londoners,* also informs Arthur Rowe's actions in *The Ministry of Fear,* once he is on the trail of fifth-columnists and spies. At that point Rowe is part of the war effort. And the war effort was shared even by his world weary creator, Graham Greene. In *Ways of Escape,* Greene links his own experience directly to the descriptions in *The Ministry of Fear*:

> I think too the atmosphere of the blitz is well conveyed. The three flares which Rowe saw come 'sailing slowly, beautifully, down, clusters of spangles off a Christmas tree, 'I had watched myself, flattened up against the wall of Manaple's store on the night of the great raid of April 16, 1941 .[13]

Part of "the atmosphere of the blitz," conveyed both in Greene's autobiographical account and countless other personal memoirs; is a sense of community and Camaraderie:

> In those days London had been a cluster of villages-one hardly ever wandered to distant places like Hampstead, or Knightsbridge...The author of *The Napoleon of Notting Hill* would have loved, those days, and so in a sense did I and my fellows wardens at our port under the school of Tropical Medicine in Gower Street. While I wrote *The Ministry of Fear* far away in West Africa a little of the love crept, I think, into the book.[14]

The love that crept into that book is different from the sort of love, both sacred and profane, that is easily accounted for in the standard view of Greenland as a moral and metaphorical battlefield. The real battlefield in 1940-41 had a surprising effect on Greene and many others like him.

Once war became a patriotic affair in Britain (after the fall of Chamberlain, followed almost at once by the invasion of the Low Countries, the fall of France and the threat of invasion), sentiment flooded English life. An excess of sentiment is normal during war, but what made 1940-41 different in Britain was that that sentiment was generally shared even by those normally cynical about such emotion. Julian Symons, then a conscientious objector, predicted the change before it occurred. In his "London letter" to the Kenyon Review of December 1939-during the listlelessness of the phoney war-he writes:

> It is axiomatic that "Common sense" has little chance in a war: and it is obvious to that inflation of language and sentiment in literature is as certain in wartime as inflation of prices... It is not difficult to see what will happen in the near future. The emotional temperature will go up, and poetry and prose will become more poetic.[15]

Although Greene did not always manage to tone down the commonplace sentiment of the time in his writing during the war, he did manage to incorporate it into the dramatic action of his fiction in his forward to *Penguin New Writing,* John Lehmann analyses the difference in mood between 1940 and 1944. He comments on the two dominant impressions he has gained from the contributions sent to him (as editor) by writers in uniform.

The first was that in almost all of them the war had become a settled condition...And the other impression arose directly from the first: that in this new way of life the writers had become aware of gulfs around them they had not imagined existed, or could ignore, in their earlier life.[2] Their sense of "division and loneliness", he argues arises out of the absence of a system of beliefs. There is no longer, in 1944,

> a myth whose wholeness would heal the wound between war and peace-time occupation, between the past and the present, between one class and another; a myth when we in England felt we were about to recapture for one moment of astonishing intensity in 1940, when everything seemed to be falling into place.[16]

The whole passage could be read as a choric comment on *The Ministry of Fear* in which Greene drew on his experience of what a direct hit was like:

> And then the bomb went off.
>
> They hadn't heard the plane this time; destruction had come drifting quietly down on green silk cords: the walls suddenly caved in. They were not even aware of noise.
>
> Blast is an odd thing; it is just as likely to have the effect of an embarrassing dream as of man's serious vengeance on man, landing you naked in the street or exposing you in your bed or on your lavatory seat to the neighbor's gaze. Rowe's head was singing; he felt as though he had been walking in his sleep; he was lying in a strange position, in a strange place. He got up and saw an enormous quantity of saucepans all over the floor: something like the twisted engine of an old car turned out to be a refrigerator...[18]

Greene's hero Rowe looks up and sees Charles's Wain (the group of seven bright stars in the Great Bear), below him a water colour intact at his feet, at his feet, and he feels as if he were in a strange country, without maps to help him, to find his position by the stars.

> Three flares came sailing slowly, beautifully, down, clusters of spangles off a Christmas tree: his shadow shot out in front of him and he felt exposed, like a gaolbreaker caught in a searchlight beam...They were machine-gunning the flares: two broke with a sound like cracking plates and the third came to earth in Russell Square; the darkness returned coldly comfortingly.
>
> But in the light of the flares Rowe had seen several things; he had discovered where he was-in the basement kitchen: the chair above his head was in his own room on the first floor, the front wall had

> gone and all the roof, and the cripple lay beside the chair, one arm swinging loosely down at him. A warden called from the street, 'Is anyone hurt in there? And Rowe said aloud in a sudden return of his rage, 'It's beyond a joke: It's beyond a joke.
>
> 'You're telling me,'the warden called down to him from the shattered street as yet another raider came up from the south-east muttering to them both like a witch in a child's dream, 'Where are you? Where are you? Where are you?[19]

Robert Greenwood's *The Squad Goes Out* is a typical blitz novel, published in 1943, the same year as *The Ministry of Fear* appeared. In it the central character is a middle-class man who is educated out of his bourgeois taboos and prejudices by serving in a Bermondsey ambulance unit with working class locals during the bombing of 1940. The ambulance is destroyed by a direct hit, and the book ends with the officer in charge of the unit looking out from his office window after the loss of its classless crew. The October mist places the scene at exactly the same historical moment as Greene's *At Home* essay.

The physical surroundings and wartime colonial ethos in which he worked on his book about the blitz were to become the setting for his next war novel, *The Heart of the Matter*. That later novel, however, published after the war in 1948, uses the contemporary scene as a backdrop, not as a force shaping the action. In this, *The Heart of the Matter* is an accurate reflector of the changed mood of the middle war years. Scobie in his West African port is simply doing his duty in another part of the map. The enforced exile of war is a feature of the life lived in his hot little town, as is the constant presence on danger in the ocean beyond the harbour.

Robert Gorham Davis, writing about the landscape and the characters in *The End of the Affair*, says:

> In Greene's novel everything is as drab and dreary as possible. London is bomb damaged; it rains all

> the time; the heroine has a bad cough; the meals are indigestible and made to sound so; the people ate boring or nerve-racking; love is described largely in physical terms, and those repellent ones. The characters turn to the Church because they find life intolerable.[20]

The eschatological and romantic elements in Greene's work are brought together in the theme of *The End of the Affair.* This is how Greene describes the pre-war summer in the novel:

> The daily newspaper, the daily meal, the traffic grinding towards Battersea, the gulls coming up from the Thames looking for bread, and the early summer of 1939 glinting on the park where children sailed their boats—one of those bright, condemned pre-war summers....drinking bad South African sherry because of the war in Spain...in those years the sense of happiness had been a long while dying under the coming storm.. .The eighteenth century church stood like a toy in an island of grass—the toy could be left outside in the dark, in the dry unbreakable weather.[21]

The past itself is recalled with the memorability of a travelogue in *The End of the Affair.* The war, the moods of its phases, and the details of action such as the first VI raid, are all presented in recollection (the narrative begins when the war is over) that resembles a voice-over script for historical film footage. In place of the immediacy of the blitz in *The Ministry of Fear,* we have Bendrix's digestion of the past. Although he concludes that his view is inevitably personal, his tone is remarkably assured. Words are after all, his trade:

> Now that I come to write my own story the problem is still the same but worse-there are so many more facts, now that I have not to invent them. How can I disinter the human character from the heavy scene-the daily newspaper, the daily meal, the traffic

> grinding towards Battersea. the gulls coming up from the Thames looking for bread, and the early summer of 1939 glinting on the park where the children sailed their boats—one of those bright condemned pre-war summers?[22]

In the first VI raid on London Bendrix is trapped under false masonary, and Sarah, begging for his return makes her vow to God. That crucial event is introduced with a short summary of the history of the bombing of London:

> It was the first night of what were later called the VIS in June 1944. We had become unused to air-raids. Apart from the short spell in February 1944, there had been nothing since the blitz petered out with the great final raids of 1941. When the sirens went and the first robots came over, we assumed that a few planes had broken through one night defence.[23]

The description shows how far *The End of the Affair* is from any direct experience of wartime moods and the values. And its distancing of the war vividly contrasts with the omnipresence of war in *The Ministry of Fear,* Greene's war novel written in wartime. Air raids are a part of the fabric of *The Ministry of Fear.* Even if not the focus of attention, the raids provide an undercurrent when, for example, guns open up outside an indoor setting which at that point holds the main narrative interest or when road-damage conditions the way a daytime London scene is experienced. But beyond the simple fact of the omnipresence of war-damage and danger, the reaction to bombing is integral to the moral ethos of the book.

In *The Ministry of Fear* Greene synthesized the overriding concerns of the first period of his writing while making a transition to the private spiritual pre-occupations that characterize his later spiritual novels. Greene thinks that the scenes in the mental clinic are the best in the novel, and the atmosphere of Blitz well conveyed. Before leaving London for Freetown he had been a fire warden on the west side of Bloomsbury and like Rowe had watched the flares wiling slowly down clusters of spangles off a Christmas tree. On the night of the Great blitz on 16 April 1941, he wrote in his journal:

> Standing on the roof of a garage we saw the flames come slowly floating down, dribbling their flames: they drift the great yellow peonies...The flares come down again right on top of us as the Pole, Miss S (of Bourne and Hollingsworth) and I stood in Tottenham Court Road at the comer of Alfred place. A white southern light: we cast long shadows and the flares come down from west to east across Charlotte Street. Then a few minutes later without the warning of a whistle, there was a huge detonation. We only had time to get on our haunchs and the shop window showered down on our helmets.[24]

He spent the rest of the night carrying the injured in their blood smeared pyjamas from RADA and the Victoria Club on Malet Street. During the Blitz Greene recorded many other incidents, some of which would surface later in his novels. Once he had to go inside a building to look for a trapped man and came on what was apparently a body: only the head and shoulders visible and a clot of blood by the head. Quiet and slumped and just a peaceful post of the rubble. The scene is reminiscent of the one in which Sarah finds Bendrix after the bombing in *The End of the Affair (1951)*. Greene later said it was while he was fire warden that he lost his fear of blood. As a child he could faint at the mention of it, but during the Blitz his sensitivity came under control as he helped the injured: "A street accident is horrible and fortuitous, but all this belonged to human nature."[25]

It was not only the comparative peace of Freetown that gave Greene's life shape after the chaos of London. Once the war began and the political situation became superficially straightforward so that things required practical rather than theoretical situations, his non-fictional writing lost its hysteria and focused with apparent ease on the war effort.

> Once the war started Greene was back at what he did best, defending the little man not interested in ideologies and bashing politicians who did nothing but create suspicion and doubts which lead the mind toward despair.[26]

Greene's writing about the World War II reflects the period in which it was written as much as the period about which it was written. The distinctively seedy, compromised and flawed milieu, setting to his pre-war fiction, was successively incorporated into this novel written during the war. In the works written after the war, energy and intoxication are replaced by world weariness consistent with both post-war concerns in a shabby, ruined divided Europe and the fatigue experienced by all in the last years of the war itself, lovingly recreates the French scene, French architecture and French customs. A sense of awe at the horrors of life in an occupied country, with the taking and execution of hostages, is submerged under the more familiar Greenland aura of Judas-like-betrayal and self-interest under stress. These elements predominate in the war-time script.

Graham Greene's knack of functioning real-life situations in different parts of the world has been the source of much of his strength as a novelist. Greene's novel *The Quiet American* (1955) has been influenced by the Vietnam War. Greene went to Vietnam several times and watched this war from close quarters. This war took place between the Vietnamese Communists and guerillas on the one hand, and the Vietnamese government, backed by the French, or the other. Ever since the division of Vietnam into two parts—North Vietnam and South Vietnam—in 1954, the guerilla forces (the Viet Cong), with the backing of North Vietnam under the communist regime of Ho Chi Minh, had been fighting against the South Vietnamese government, America had come to help South Vietnam in so-called anti-Communist drive and was engaged in a massive battle with the Viet Cong forces. Greene, who had an opportunity of witnessing the Vietnamese's political situation, has presented the struggle which culminated in the defeat of the French, in *The Quiet American*. Like so many of Greene's novels, *The Quiet American* was inspired by his personal experience of a particular part of the world. He has translated into the novel his experiences as the Indo-China correspondent of *Life* and the *London Sunday Times in the Fifties*. Greene has said in a B B C talk:

> And of course, there is a coincidence about Indo-China. I went there because there was a war on and I stayed there for every winter for four years to watch a war. And out of that a novel emerged.[27]

The Indo-China of the novel is yet another uncomfortable corner of Greenland. The images here also evoke the atmosphere of seediness and decay. The Vietnamese Surete in Saigon, like the police station in Scobie's Africa, smells of urine and injustice. The atrocities and suffering caused by the war are made vivid through Fowler's reactions. Captain Trouin tells him about a girl in Hanoi:

> There was a girl in the mortuary-they had not only cut off her breasts, they had mutilated her lover and stuffed his...They find a mother and child who were caught in the line of fire in a narrow ditch: They were very clearly dead; a small neat clot of blood on the woman's forehead, and the child might have been sleeping. He was about six years old and he lay like an embryo the womb with his little bony knees drawn up ...There was a gnawed piece of loaf under his body. I thought I hate war.[28]

It is a political novel-or parable about the war in Indo-China employing its characters less as individuals than as representatives of their nations or political factions. Greene tells a complex but compelling story of intrigue and counter-intrigue, bombing and murder. Into it is mixed the rivalry of two white men for a Vietnamese girl. These elements are all subordinate to the political thesis which they dramatize and which is stated badly and explicitly throughout the book. As the title suggests, America is the principal concern. The thesis is quite simply that America is crassly materialistic with no understanding of other peoples. In *The Quiet American* the effect of circumstances is specifically ideological and political. Everything that the British reporter, Fowler, sees of the war, of the indiscriminate slaughter of civilians, drives him out of his uninvolvidness towards a decision. In this novel, a murderous outrage occurs, intended to affect the war's course. A badly timed bombing in the public square of Saigon, planned to disrupt a parade, instead kills mostly women and children. The novel is dominated by death, so much so that Conor Cruise O'Brien calls it the fourth character in the story (the other three being Fowler, Phuong and Pyle). Fowler's anger and pity are Greene's. Nowhere is this more apparent than in the scene where Fowler goes with Captain Trouin on a bombing mission. They drop napalm bombs on a village and leave it burning. As they return, they blow up a sampan and Fowler, the observer, reflects:

> There had been something so shocking in our sudden fortuitous choice of a prey-we had just happened to be passing; one burst only was required, there was no one to return our fire, we were gone again, adding our little quota to the world's dead: on their way back, Captain Trouin, like a gracious host, shows Fowler the wonderful sunset: The helmeted martin face looked wistfully out, down the golden groves among the great humps and arches of porous stone and the wound of murder ceased to bleed.[29]

The ironical contrast between Captain Trouin's civility as a host and the savagery of what he has just done implies Greene's angry comment on the inhumanity of the civilized world. In the context of the whole novel, one finds in this sunset an infernal quality, the lurid glow of a hell where the poor devils are burned alive, the flames go over them like water. They are wet through fire. The representative character of Fowler is highly individualized character, a typical Greene hero, whose nature is compounded of all those traits which signify Greene's unceasing preoccupation with flawed human beings.

The Quiet American, which exposed the CIA involvement with terrorist attacks on civilians in Vietnam, was left in limbo for over 12 months due to September 11 episode, and was then only released in selected cities for a short season after public pressure from its British star Michael Caine. *The Quiet American* raises serious questions about the CIA's collaboration with local terrorists in Vietnam who staged attacks on innocent civilians as part of a Machiavellian plan to hasten regime change as the communists in the North were quickly gaining ground against the French colonial rulers. Alden Pyle, the young ideologue and undercover CIA agent, is driven by a burning yet paternalistic desire to save the Vietnamese from the threat of communism through any means. He believes in mobilizing a democratic 'third force' that will transform Asia and prevent it from falling into the grip of the communists. He is a product both of his time and of his own youthful ardour. Pyle's liberationist rhetoric is remarkably similar to the language of the Bush administration on Iraq. There was something bizarre, indeed surreal, about George W. Bush's recent reference to Graham Greene's novel *The Quiet American* in his speech to the National Convention of the Veterans of Foreign Wars. Attempting to draw a parallel between the conflict in Vietnam and the current conflagration in Iraq, Bush criticized Greene's suggestion that the "quiet American's" patriotism was dangerously naive:

> In 1955...Graham Greene wrote a novel called *The Quiet American.* It was set in Saigon, and the main character was a young government agent named

> Alden Pyle. He was a symbol of American purpose and patriotism—and dangerous naivete.[30]

Like most of his generation of writers Greene had spent his early years in Edwardian middle-class comfort, and he lived through the two world wars. In his earliest memories Greene is nostalgic for the relative peace and security of that world. In 1924, five years before Greene's first novel was published, and while he was an undergraduate at Oxford, he read a book of short stories by Geoffrey Moss called *Defeat*. It was about the occupied Rhineland. In it Moss described the "atrocitious conduct of the French troops at Trier...where they were trying to set up a little separatist republic in order to divide Germany."[31]

Greene's visit to the Rhineland, which he made with Claud Cockburn in the spring of 1924 against his father's strong objections, came at the end of a bizarre and dangerous period in his life in which he played Russian roulette first on Berkhamstead Common in the autumn of 1923, later several times on a country road near Oxford. In *The Name of Action (1930)*, Greene was drawing on his limited but firsthand knowledge of the Rhineland. Like Greene's early heroes, Oliver Chant is a middle-class Englishman disenchanted with his own world and a life without meaning in England. In search of commitment, he offers money and support to an exile from the Ruhr who visits him in London and who is connected to a group of rebels in Trier. The book is set after the French have left the Rhineland, sometime in the late twenties. Its mission, when Chant joins it, is to overthrow the Dictator, Demassener, whom the group hopes to overthrow. Greene makes an attempt to get off a few final charges against the occupiers of Rhineland.

> All the scum of Europe was there, Demassener tells tells Chant. The caparets were nothing but filth... [it was] a sexual debauch.[32]

Although Greene used the city of Trier as a backdrop, yet he had to rely heavily for his story on the more personal theme of betrayal. As far as the plot goes the betrayals are straightforward: Chant deceives Demassener by sleeping with his wife; she betrays her husband by telling Chant the Dictator is impotent; Chant tells the rebels; they tell the entire city and sway public opinion against Demassener. The world Greene describes is irrational. Nothing is fixed or predictable and Chant seeks with an adolescent desperation, some "clear beliefs round which to form his words."[33]

What Chant finds is that the old idealisms he has come to Trier to fight for, justice, loyalty and purpose, are emptied of meaning. He leaves without the certainty he sought for himself of a specific function in an ordered world. Although the above novel does not reflect its times in the sense that Evelyn Waugh's first novel *Decline and Fall (1928}* did, where Paul Penny Feather tells Lord Circumference that he is sure there is going to be another war. Nevertheless, in both *The Name of Action* and *Rumour at Nightfall,* political struggle was central and when Greene's settings did switch to the present in 1932 with *Stamboul Train,* very quickly the possibility of a second European war filled his writing with a sense of crisis. T.S.Eliot marked the year of the General Strike as the point at which the:

> Features of the post-war world began clearly to emerge...From about that date, he said, 'One began slowly to realize that the intellectual and artistic output of the previous seven years had been rather the last efforts of an world than the struggles of a new.[34]

Greene took his direction for *Stamboul Train* from the movie *Grand Hotel.* Greene's desire to produce a popular novel influenced the style of *Stamboul Train,* a contemporary thriller in which the dialogue is more dramatic than in his earlier books. But it is something else in the novel which marks, in Greene's work, that point

Eliot noted more generally at which the features of the post-war world came into focus. In *Stamboul Train* Greene called into question the values he grew up with and began to discuss how to act in the face of their collapse. From then to the end of the decade, war became a constant and complex in his books. His characters were engaged in a social battle, though it was far from the Marxist notion of a close war. In *It's a Battlefield,* for example, the rally against the Means Test held in Hyde Park in 1932 Czinner is killed outside England by foreign hands. In 1934 Jim Drover is reprieved. His brother dies in London, but accidentally. In 1935 Tony is murdered, against outside England. As Europe darkens, however, corruption and violence pervade the entire social structure of the books so that in 1936 when Raven is hired by people in high places to assassinate a socialist minister on the Continent, Europe is brought to the brink of war.

The 1938 violence and profiteering are rampant in Greene's novels. The class war in England, represented by the struggles between Raven and Sir Marcus, Pinkie and Colleoni, is assimilated to the war that looms on the continent. The real threat here is not the system itself but the disorder within it that arose, Greene implies, when the values of liberal humanism fell to those of monopoly capitalism. The fact that the idea of responsibility for society and its regeneration is foreign to Greene's upper-class figures is a measure of his pessimism about that disorder. The threat in these novels is disorder, and the characters who lead in that direction, whether criminals, social misfits or revolutionaries, are punished.

In 1939, in *The Confidential Agent* England is again described as a battlefield. The protagonists in the novels of 1930s lack faith, not in man's goodness but in man's reason and, hence, in the future. Czinner, Drover, Anthony and Rove are well intentioned good men but they sit in an untenable position. They cannot accept injustice and chaos of their society; they cannot return to what they consider a safer time like the protagonists of Greene's earlier romances, a past they have, in any case, sentimentalized; and they cannot welcome a future they believe will be worse than the present. This is not a failure of man's goodness, but of his courage. These characters are society's victims and they are also Greene's. They are the product of his own sense of impotence as he watches capitalism stagger from crisis to crisis, while he sees no clear direction in which to proceed. This novel is written against the background of the Spanish Civil War and presents the conflict between the capitalist world of monopoly and proflt and the socialist world of struggle, equality and poverty. It tells the story of a loyalist agent D. Sent to England by the government of a country torn by Civil War, to procure coal for his side. In England, he undergoes a nightmarish experience of intrigue, violence and corruption, and is subjected to violence by the criminals hired by the enemy agent L. He falls in love with Rose Cullen, daughter of Lord Benditch, with whom he has come to strike a coal-deal. D. is not successful in getting coal for his side, but he prevents the other side from procuring it. Finally, he escapes from that country and comes back to England accompanied by his beloved, Rose.

A Gun For Sale was published in July 1936, the same month the Spanish Civil War began. In it, Raven is hired by Sir Marcus, an English armament manufacturer, to murder a socialist minister of a foreign state so that war would be forced on Europe and his trade stimulated. The plot, like most of Greene's novels of this period, was structured around a manhunt. Raven is sought by the police and by Sir Marcus, who does not want to be associated with the assassination. Greene took his direction for the novel from two current publications: Sir Marcus was suggested by a biography of Sir Basil Zaharoff, the armaments King, and a situation by a report from a Royal Commission looking into the manufacture and sale of arms. The novel is about violence and approaching war. Greene sustains an atmosphere of doom on several levels. The possibility of war is about in newspapers, shouted out by newsboys, spoken of on radio, and practised for in an air-raid drill. This atmosphere of battle is reinforced by the bleakness of the setting. The countryside through which Anne's train passes and Nottwich itself are described as fields of battle holding images of the social war between the moneyed and powerful and the poor and rejected. Within this setting, Raven fights for his personal war against the poverty of his background and the scars left by his mother's suicide. As an individual he is similar to the world Greene has created. Raven kills for money as the world, run by the likes of Sir Marcus, starts wars for commercial reasons. Raven comes to trust Anne but she betrays him, and he dies in the unbearable pain of what he always believed: "You could trust no one, not a doctor, not a priest, not a woman."[35]

The war has been postponed, but it will happen as surely as Raven is betrayed. "Men were fighting, beasts, they needed war... They love it."[36] Anne thinks as she stares out of her train window "at the bleak-frozen countryside"[37] on the way back to London. And in the final recognition of the battle lost, Greene adds: "Perhaps even if she had been able to save the country from war, it wouldn't have been worth the saving."[38] As Greene described in great detail what he saw in Paris in 1934 to invoke the experience of the strike, so in *A Gun For Sale* he used a myriad of details to impregnate the setting with a feeling of the present. The power of the book is in Greene's ability to have the atmosphere of violence, fear and threatening doom reflect, not analyze, the psychological condition of being besieged.

In 1940, in *Time and Tide,* Greene wrote about getting used to war:

> Violence comes more easily because it was so long expected-not only by the political sense but by the moral sense. The world we lived in could not have ended any other way. The curious waste lands one sometimes say from the trains-the created ground

> round Wolverhampton under a cindery sky with a few cottages grouped like stones among the rubbish: those acres of abandoned cars round Slough; the dingy fortune tellers on the fire-floor above the cheap permanent waves in a Brighton back street: they all demanded violence, like the rooms in a dream where one knows that something will permanently happen-a door fly open or a window-catch give and let the end in.[39]

The writers of his generation, he noted, had gone abroad to meet violence hall way:

> Some went to Spain and others to China. Less ideological. perhaps less courageous, writers chose corners where the violence was more moderate; but the hint of it had to be there to satisfy that moral craving for the just and reasonable expression of human nature left without belief. The craving wasn't quite satisfied because we all bought two-way tickets. Like Henry James hearing a good story at a dinner-table we could say, Stop. That's enough for our purpose, and take a train or a boat at home. The moral sense was tickled: that was all. One came home and wrote a book, leaving the condemned behind...All the same -egotistical to the last—we can regard those journeys as a useful rehearsal.[40]

Greene waited under the London pavement while the bombs fell overhead. "If a cracked cup is put in boiling water it breaks, and an old dog-toothed civilization is breaking now."[41]

War had come out of the shabby depressed world he had rightly seen as symptomic of the crisis of his culture. Whether in England or in Mexico his view of society had been simple. It included two classes, the oppressors and the victims. A full political engagement came to Greene more gradually, after his suspicion that nothing could remedy the social breakdown of Europe. The chaos prevalent in Spain, Russia and Mexico confirmed his belief that revolutions may make things worse than they are. Hope vanished with the war: "Hope, the whisky priest said, is an instinct only the reasoning human mind can kill."[42] Stalin's Russia, Spain and Mexico proved to Greene that man's reasoning was lethal.

In a sense *The Power and the Glory* is his *1984*. The book is a powerful picture of a world in which man has done his best to destroy the individuality and freedom of his fellow man. On the one hand, it shows the revolution gone wrong, the hope for a better world dashed in violence and draws the conclusion that after all, the end was along the pavement all along. Man reared in a waste land cannot be expected to do better. On the other hand, it is individual transcendence through Catholicism. Greene thought as he waited in London for the bombs to fall:

> Life has become just and poetic, and if we believe this is the right end to the muddled thought; the sentimentality and selfishness of generations, we can also believe that justice does not end there The innocent will be given their peace, and the unhappy will know more happiness than they have ever dreamt about, and poor muddled people will be given an answer they have to accept. We needn't feel pity for any of the innocent, and as for the guilty. We know in our hearts that they will live just as along as we do and no longer.[43]

Flawed man, flawed world were under the pavement all the time. Many people lying at night on a cement floor in the company of total strangers must catch themselves dreaming of some other period of history in which they would prefer to have lived. The book by Sir Compton Mackenzie[44], *Sinister Street* suggested the collapse of that whole way of life. As Greene read the book, he found it rather horrifying. Again and again we are left with Greene's resignation as he seems to clearly see that human progress had been an illusion and the war had to happen. A historian might say that he was caught in an ideological crisis over the collapse of liberal humanism, a psychiatrist might find that he was depressed and a catholic could say that he was a Jansenist. Greene himself said that he had simply accepted "that all the while the end of things-as we know them-is coming."[45] Greene's generation had expected war any time and Greene had marked it. Coming in the wastelands of England, yet he could find no way to explain human virtue which remained despite the violence of the visible world. As an artist he could resolve the conflict or achieve a synthesis, in the paradoxical and inexplicable- the idealistic lieutenant who stifled room life from the best possible motives, the drunken priest who continued to pass life on-but as a journalist he could not explain it. While Greene waited under the London pavement for the bombs to be dropped by, he thought about what could be explained by environment and what could not. Before the war he had used the shabby detritus of the modem city to mirror the state of individual conscience. As war began, he decided that "fidelity and the courage of human beings abandoned to free will"[46] could only be included as inexplicable. The material experience of life could not explain them. They had to be lumped in with the religious experience and resolved aesthetically. This is not to say that Greene exaggerated, either as a novelist or as a reporter. Exaggeration was abhorrent to him, and he resents being accused of it. Some critics have referred to a strange violent seedy region of the mind which they call Greenland:

> This is Indo-China, I want to exclaim, this is Mexico, this is Sierra Leone carefully and accurately described. I have been a newspaper correspondent as well as a novelist...But I know the argument is useless. They won't believe the world they haven't noticed is like that.[47]

In *The Third Man,*, Graham Greene gives expression to his impatience with the Cold War politics of the time by refusing to take an ideological stance on either side.

Instead, he offers a parody of the Cold War, as Rollo Martins turns Old Vienna into the American Old West in his search for the killers of his hero, Harry Lime. Heroes and hero worship are parodied in *The Third Man.* The emphasis on "Westerns" in it provides an oblique reference to the Cold War. A dominant theme of "westerns" is "the conflict of East and West-or, more precisely, the conflict between the values symbolized by the East and those symbolized by the West This theme of East versus West, or "civilisation versus the primitive", suggests a parody of the Cold War conflict of Western ideology and Communist ideology.

Greene expresses his dissatisfaction with the dehumanizing tendencies of war not only in his novels but also in one of his short stories, *The Destructors.* It is a short story which is universal in its reflection of human nature. In it, the theme of destruction is discussed through various symbolic characters and objects. Greene has effectively reflected on the destructions caused by wars and conflict, by scaling a full scale holocaust of a nation to a localized full scale vandalisation by the Wormsley Common Gang. The story contains many of Greene's hallmarks, most importantly that of placing people who have the capacity for good and evil in situations where they must make a choice between the two. The boys in *The Destructors* are still young enough to be innocent, yet they make cruel and selfish choices. This story is also a link to Greene's earliest fiction in which he often portrayed young people being initiated into the adult world. Commenting on this story and three others ("A Chance for Mr. Lever," "Under the Garden," and "Cheap in August"), Greene declared that he was completely satisfied and had never written anything better.

The Destructors occurs in the mid-1950s, and is about a boys' gang named the "Wormsley Common Gang", after the place where they live. Trevor, or "T", the protagonist, devises a plan to destroy a two hundred-year-old house that survived The Blitz, simply because it is beautiful.

Under T, their new leader, the gang accepts the plan and executes it when the owner of the house, Mr. Thomas (whom the gang call "Old Misery"), is away during a bank holiday weekend. Their plan is to destroy the house from inside, then tear down the remaining infrastructure. Mr. Thomas returns home early, however, and the gang locks him in the outhouse and completes the destruction of his house and home. Gang leader T refuses to stop until the destruction job is complete, because even the facade is valuable and could be reused. The final damage to the house is done when a parked lorry pulls away a support pole from the side of the house. Mr. Thomas is released from the outhouse from aforementioned lorry's driver and is left with the dusty rubble of what once was his home.

References

1. W. Warren Wagar. *A Short History of the Future.* Chicago: University of Chicago Press, 1989.
2. Mary Shelley. *The Last Man.* Lincoln, Neb University of Nebraska Press. 1965.
3. J. Eric Hobsbawm. *Primitive Rebels: Studies in Archaic Forms of Social Movement in the Nineteenth and Twentieth Centuries.* New York: Norton, 1965, p.57.
4. Arthur Kroker and David Cook. The *Postmodern Scene: Excremental Culture and Hyper-Aesthetics.* New York: St. Martin's Press, 1986, p.8-9.
5. Daniel Wojcik. *The End of the World As We Know It: Faith, Fatalism and Apocalypse in America.* New York: New York University Press, 1997,
6. Frank Kermode. *The Sense of an Ending.* London: Oxford University Press, 1974.
7. Graham Greene. *Ways of Escape.* London: Bodely Head, 1980, p. 146.
8. Graham Greene. *Collected Essays.* London: Bodley Head, 1969, p. 17.
9. Richard Hoggert. *Auden: An Introductory Essay.* London: Chatto & Windus, 1951, p.45.

10. Morton Dauwen Zabel. *Graham Greene: The Best and the Worst in Craft and Character*. London: Gollancz, 1957, p. 30-31.
11. Graham Greene. *The Ministry of Fear*. London: Heinemann, 1943, p. 31.
12. Graham Greene. 'At Home', *Collected Essays*. London: Bodley Head, 1983, p.450.
13. *Ways of Escapes*, p. 81.
14. *Ways of Escapes*, p. 81-82.
15. Quoted in Julian Symons. *Notes from another Country*. Oxford: Oxford University Press, 1972, p.67.
16. John Lehman. *Penguin New Writing*. London: Penguin New Writing,1944, p.19.
17. Lehmann, 1944, p. 7.
18. *The Ministry of Fear*, p. 28.
19. *The Ministry of Fear*, p.64
20. Quoted in Francis Brown. *Highlights of Modern literature*. New York: New American Library, 1954, p. 60.
21. Graham Greene. *The End of the Affair*. London: Heinemann, 1975, p.25-6.
22. *The end of the Affair*, p. 22.
23. *The End of the Affair*, pp. 71-72.
24. *Ways of Escapes*, p. 89.
25. *Ways of Escape*. P. 91.
26. Graham Greene. *The Lost Childhood and Other Essays*. London: Heinemann, 1951, p. 646.
27. A.S. Raman. *The Illustrated Weekly of India*. 19 January. 1964, p.21.
28. Graham Greene. *The Quiet American. London*: Heinemann, 1955, pp.62-63.
29. *The Quiet American*, pp. 62-63.
30. Joseph Pearce. "The Unquiet Graham Greene" *The American Conservative*, October 22, 2007, 99. 65-73.
31. Marie Francoise Allian. *The Other Man: Conservations with Graham Greene*. London: Bodley, 1983, p.39.

32. Graham Greene. *The Name of Action*. New York: Dombleday, 1931, p.58.
33. Graham Greene. *Rumour at Nightfall*. London: Heinemarm, 1931, p.64.
34. T.S. Eliot. "Last Words" *The Criterion*. 18 January 1939, pp 271-276.
35. Graham Greene. *A Gun For Sale*. London: Heinemann, 1936, p. 48.
36. *A Gun For Sale*, p. 113.
37. *A Gun For Sale*, p. 172.
38. *A Gun For Sale*, p. 187.
39. Graham Greene. *Notes on the Way: Time and Tide*. 19 October, p. 100
40. *Notes on the Way: Time and Tide*, p. 102.
41. *Notes on the Way: Time and Tide*, p. 121.
42. Graham Greene. *The Power and the Glory*. London: Heinemannm, 1940, pp. 141-2.
43. *The Power and the Glory*, p. 143.
44. Sir Compton Mackenzie. *Sinister. London*, Arkham House, 1967.
45. *The Power and the Glory*, p. 146.
46. *The Power and the Glory*, p. 156.
47. *Ways of Escapes*, p. 60.

4

Backdrop to Structural Forms

Jerry H. Bryant in his book *The Open Decision*[1] *writes* that the critics of the post-war era complained that the American novel projected the portrait of man as an ignominious insect, cowering and helpless without his old God. It also shows man as an aimless and purposeless victim of biological and social forces over which he has no control and it shows a sensitive creature too delicate for this world, plunged in a melancholy gloom of alienation, estrangement, angst and despair. The argument of the critics seems valid as the contemporary literature does seem to depict man in a state of crisis of identity. This stands true not only to American novel but British also, and Graham Greene is one such writer who is acutely conscious of this Godless universe. As argued in the previous two chapters that Greene's apocalyptic outlook was shaped by many factors and World War I was one of them the two world wars had their evil effects also which got manifested in the literature of those times. Hence Greene reflects in his novels the dominant theme that our universe is absurd, chaotic and without meaning life during and after the wars, became absolutely meaningless and purposeless. Man started questioning, the very existance of God. Spirituality, sterlity, moral degeneration, loss of faith in christians dogmas, loss of perspective, nihilism, depression, despair, loss of direction and loss of identity are some of the characteristics features of the post war world.

All the protagonists not only in his war novels but also secular novels are cast in an alien universe, and they also are victims of many factors over which they have no control. Greene is also preoccupied with sense of crisis, angst, despair, alienation and estrangement which pervade his novels and which form a major theme of this chapter. In the apocalyptic world of *The Bible*, the Day of Judgment will be preceded by the last-loosening of Satan and this will be manifested in different forms and guises. The factors mentioned above could also be taken as the different manifestations of Satan. The end of the world as prophesied in *The Bible* will also be preceded by the general moral and physical degradation of human and spiritual values and these factors also link Greene with the tradition of apocalypse. In addition, eschatological beliefs, that is, beliefs about the end of the world, also pervade the novels of Greene. However, Greene is peculiar in his approach in that he is not only obsessed with these apocalyptic themes but his themes correspond to his settings and vice versa. The imagery that he uses in his novels could be compared to the demonic imagery in contrast to the apocalyptic imagery of the heavenly world of *The Bible.* Many modern novelists present the contemporary civilization in terms of this demonically parodied world. Northup Frye calls this type of parody of apocalyptic imagery as demonic imagery.[2] It is primarily in the light of these factors that an attempt will be made to highlight Greene as an apocalyptic novelist.

Graham Greene writes in his autobiography, *A Sort of Life:* if I were to choose an epigraph for all novels I have written, it would be from *Bishop Bloughram 's Apology:*

> Our interest is on the dangerous edge of things,
> The honest thief, the tender murderer,
> The superstitious atheist, demi-rep

That loves and saves her soul in new French books-
We watch while these in equilibrium keep
The giddy line midway.[3]

The situations that Greene has chosen for his novels have provided him with the materials of melodrama; his imagination finds its expression in wars and revolutions, and among criminals and police, the hunters and the hunted. These are materials that our world provides in abundance, life in the twentieth century is melodramatic. But he has not written melodrama for its own sake; he has used it to furnish his world with the texture of violence, terror and cruelty that he finds in life. As mentioned in the second chapter. Greene is obsessed with the inhuman character of humanity. His settings have been so consistently vivid and actual that they have been given a collective name—"Greenland"-and a descriptive adjective—"seedy." Greene objects to both the noun and the adjective, but he can scarcely deny that his world is consistently seedy, sordid, violent and cruel. These qualities are part of the legend: they describe not an actual environment, but an image of a spiritual condition—a world abandoned by God. A Crooner in *A Gun for Sale* sang of Greenland, thus encouraging critics to talk of 'Greenland'.[4] Whether the fictional locations were Brighton or Mexico, London or Liberia, Vietnam or Sierra Leone, Greene transformed them into Greenland: a distinctively blighted, tainted, oppressive landscape. Greene repeatedly sought to render warfare, oppression, crisis, vice and squalor. In *Journey Without Maps* he acknowledged the deep appeal of the seedy. These seedy settings and gloomy atmosphere of Greenland reflect flying bleak vision, the vision that depicts and laments the modern wasteland of Spirit. Greene is conscious of secular manifestations of apocalypse and his secular works reveal clear influence of Christian tradition that envisages corruption in all spheres in the last days. All traditions assert that corruption will overtake all spheres. In Greenland secular manifestations of evil are evident. The death of God that Nietzsche announced deeply affects modern literature. This is essentially an apocalyptic enunciation. Modern literature, in a way, is a literature of apocalypse. The death of God implies the death of meaning, order, objectivity, truth, telos, God, traditionally grounded goodness, beauty, truth, justice, virtue and all values. All these values are questioned in apocalyptic times. The world bereft of all these saving virtues is depicted in the seedy world, world bereft of grace is light, world abandoned by god, world that crushes rather than uplifts individual, world moving perpetually towards death/doom. God is an image of wholeness and fulfillment. Modem man is condemned to live as an orphan, alienated from God and thus from the depths of his self. Superficiality, triviality, meaningless pursuits, diversions, vain ego, games and traps, shallow and fragmented life of desires—all fill Greenland and are manifestations of apocalypse.

The Brighton of *Brighton Rock* has vulgar opulence, tawdry amusements, dog-muck on pavements, rusting prams in front Gardens, murder and corruption among the holiday-makers. When the moon shines in at Pinkie's window, it's the moon of Greenland; it shines on the door where the jerry stood, seeking out the chamber pot. This is how Pinkie's honeymoon with Rose begins at his lodgings:

> A smell of cabbages and cooking and burnt cloth hung about the dark passage. He nodded—'that was old Spicer's room. Do you believe in ghosts? 'I don't know.'
>
> He pushed open his own door and switched on the naked dusty light. 'There,' he said, 'take it or leave it,' and drew aside to expose the big brass bed, the washstand and chipped ewer, the varnished wardrobe with its cheap glass front. 'It's better than a hotel,' she said, 'it's more like home.'[5]

In many of his novels and tales, particularly those of the late 1930s and the 1940s, Greene's descriptive emphasis on blighted landscapes as the setting for blighted lives gave an apocalyptic flavor to his works. The pye-dogs and vultures, the slums and their refuse, the harlots and weary priests-all become predictably obedient entourage to the author on his imaginative travels. The various details in the characteristic descriptions of Greenland may all be found in reality; what matters is his recurrent emphasis on them and his elision of more positive and life-enhancing features. And, though distinctive, such descriptions can be related to various traditions. Here, for example, is a famous source of that adjective 'seedy':

> How weary, stale, flat and unprofitable
> Seem to me all the uses of this world!
> Fie on't, ah fie, 'tis an unweeded garden
> That grows to seed; things rank and gross in nature
> Possess it merely.[6]

Greene's characteristic work can also be related to the poetic tradition of urban realism and decadence. He admired Baudelaire's poems as well as Eliot's, and the 'decadent' poets of the 1890s had often enough depicted the city as a location of both squalor and corruption. Decadents gave prostitution and sexual deviance new prominence in literature. A characteristic aspect of Greenland is the frequency with which prostitutes, brothels, promiscuous women, deviant adults and even depraved children appear. Greenland sometimes implies a despairing form of romanticism, a regret for an Eden blighted. At its darkest, it evokes that Manichean sense of a world almost entirely conquered by the evil or the negative. The human characters variously fit that landscape.

As discussed in the previous chapter that the destruction caused by several wars had gone so deep in his mind that he could not exorcise the ghost of war which continued to influence his settings in one way or the other.

It found its outlet in different forms in his works. In the previous chapter we learnt how Greene expresses the dystopian vision in his treatment of the reality of war. The novels under analysis here -*Brighton Rock, The Power and the Glory, The Heart of the Matter, A Burnt-Out Case, The Human Factor and The End of the Affair*-share many features with one another which accounts for Greene's preoccupation with the seedy and sordid settings and also his themes. Part of the success of these six novels is due to the preliminary sketching of elements in each of them-a process that as it turned out, managed to release the special energy and vision that would characterize Greene as a writer of stature. The settings of *The Power and the Glory* and *The Heart of the Matter*, for example, had already been explored by Greene personally and in two excellent travel books: *The Lawless Roads*, from which whole passages are transcribed in the former; and *Journey Without Maps*, which concludes on the Gold Coast of poor Major Scobie. In the travel books, Greene's journalistic and photographic abilities exhausted themselves; and in the novels, consequently, physical settings could be managed so as to exude a meaning that transformed them into spiritual situations, into elaborated images of fate. Mexico, however discoloured, is still Mexico in *The Lawless Roods*; in *The Power and the Glory*, the country has been reduced and reshaped to fit a particular action, of which indeed it contains the particular secret. Similarly, each one of these six novels has its correlative entertainment; a mystery story in the popular sense, that functions ably as trial run for a mystery drama in a more ancient and geological sense. What Greene has envisaged and what he has become especially concerned with are better implied in the title of still another book, *It's a Battlefield*-the human scene now described as a battlefield between transcendent warring forces. In this novel, the background in its seediness becomes a part of the lives of the characters. There are shabby basement flats with hair combings as large as a baby's skull, rooms with stale air and dead bats on the floor, brothels which grow like mushrooms, factories where girls stand between death and disfigurement, prisons with A, B and C blocks which remind one of the circles of hell, evening papers which report the latest developments in the Streatham Rape and Murder case, political meetings and schisms, riots, and suppression, young tinted faces of women, overworked and without any future, giggling and chattering through dust and dark and degradation. Greene creates, like T.S.Eliot in his early poems, a waste land, a world of material poverty and spiritual emptiness. We are brought up against a whole series of persons who suffer from what Mathew Arnold called this strange disease of modern life. The London of *It's a Battlefield* is a metropolitan Hell, a place without joy or peace, love or light. The novel which springs to mind while reading *It's a Battlefield,* according to John Atkins, is Conrad's *The Secret Agent:*

> The same sordidness, the same bitterness and dark intensity runs through both of them, there is the same sense of defeat, of hopelessness, despite the occasional expressions or implications of hope.[7]

Greene was at this stage utterly hopeless about humanity, and saw man as the helpless victim of a conjunction of inner impulsions and external circumstances, with no faith to support him. One fails to notice the occasional expressions or implications of hope in a novel with such a deeply pessimistic reading of life. And in *Brighton Rock,* the metaphor of the battlefield is dominant: "It lay there always, the ravaged and disputed territory between eternities."[8]

The three novels published between 1938 and 1948 are sometimes taken together as a trilogy but the word should be enclosed in quotation marks, for the trilogic pattern, if it existed in Greene's awareness, took hold only belatedly. But it is worth juxtaposing the three books, to observe several striking aspects of Greene. All the three show his affection for the primitive. Greene often turns away from the relatively civilized to inspect human life in its cruder and more exposed conditions-in a dark corner of Brighton, the jungles and prisons of conditions, the coast of West Africa—all places where, as Scobie tells himself in *The Heart of the Matter,* 'human nature hasn't had time to disguise itself'; places where there openly flourished 'the injustices, the cruelties, the meanness that elsewhere people so cleverly hushed up'. In these primitive scenes, we encounter the dramatis personae of Greene's recurring drama and of his troubled universe-the murderer, the priest, and the policeman, who are the heroes respectively of the three books. Pinkie's Brighton is not a town or a background but a furry-driven situation, and he is involved immediately with evil and catastrophe. The world of Pinkie and Hale is also a battlefield, but with a difference:

> Good and evil lived together in the same country, spoke the same language, came together like old friends, feeling the same completion, touching hands beside the iron bedstead...[their] world lay there always, the ravaged and disputed territory between two eternities. They faced each other as it were from opposing territories, but like troops at Christmas time they fraternized.[10]

'Heaven lies about us in our infancy!' declares Wordsworth's 'Immortality Ode'. Greene's *Brighton Rock* says of Pinkie: 'Hell lay about him in his infancy.'[11] According to Cedrick Watts,[12] One of the distinctive features of Greene's life was his readiness to seek and find the ominous and the dangerous, sometimes the hellish amid the ordinary and the horrific within the mundane. *Brighton Rock* is a simple elegant thriller. Ida Arnold, the heroine, pursues the gangster Pinkie Brown: she seeks his punishment while trying to save, from his influence, the young woman, Rose, whom Pinkie has married to buy her silence. This novel is also considered to be a serious fiction, or a "modern classic". The seven sections of the book dramatize one by one an inversion of all or most of the seven sacraments-dramatize what we might call the seven deadly sacraments. This novel is probably the most striking, provocative and extreme; it is corrosively negative, grotesquely nightmarish, and cynically black-comical. It is a thriller, a detective-novel and a moral-cum-theological paradox. It offers realism, expressionism and satiric stylization. In this novel the central thematic tension is between the ethical and the religious outlooks. The concepts of right and wrong are challenged by the concepts of Good and Evil. Charles Fred is murdered by Pinkie and his gang, though the inquest wrongly adduces a verdict of death by natural causes. Ida Arnold, a Londoner, who had befriended Hale, is suspicious of the circumstances and investigates. Endeavouring to protect Rose from Pinkie, she pursues him, saves Rose from suicide and brings about destruction of Pinkie. Ida feels that a good job has been well done-a double killer has been punished. In her view, 'right' has prevailed over 'wrong'. In the character of Pinkie, Greene seems to be conducting a taxing literary experiment-to see how far the reader's pity can be won for a person who seems to be irredeemably evil and monstrously callous. The ruthless cunning of this teenage gangster is starkly depicted-his sadistic quality is carried to almost ludicrous extremes. 'She loves me...she loves me not',[13] he says, tearing the wings and legs off a fly. He wields a razor, carries a vitriol bottle, and jests crudely over his victims. He is a Judas to Spicer, his accomplice, and even to Rose, who is determinedly loyal to him even though she knows his wickedness.

Perhaps, the most insidious part of the special pleading on behalf of Pinkie is implicit in the narrator's descriptions. Pinkie's disgust at life seems largely to be shared by the narrator in his repeated observations of the tawdriness, the sleaziness and the drabness of the world. 'Why, this is Hell, nor are we out of it'[14], says Prewitt, misquoting the words of Mephistophilis in Marlowe's *Doctor Faustus*, and the narrator gives potent support to the near

Manichean sense of the hellish lurking beneath the superficial pleasures and distractions of Brighton. Expressionist art is characterized by the use of distortions which evoke a deranged or unbalanced state of mind. The accumulation of pessimistically skewed descriptive set-pieces gives *Brighton Rock* a distinctly expressionist heightening. When Pinkie returns to his home area, Paradise Piece, this is the scene:

> [T]here he was, on the top o the hill, in the thick of the bombardment a flapping gutter, [glassless] windows, an iron bedstead in a front garden the size of a table-top. Half Paradise Piece had been torn up as if by bomb-bursts; the children played about the steep slope of rubble.. .His home was gone: a flat place among the rubble may have marked its hearth; the room at the bend of the stars where the Saturday night exercise had taken place was now just air. He wondered with horror whether it all had to be built again for him; it looked better as air...
>
> The children were scouting among the rubble with pistols from Woolworth's; a group of girls surlily watched. A child with its leg in an iron brace limped blindly into him; he pushed it off; someone said in a high treble: 'Suck 'em up.' They took his mind back and he hated them for it; it was like the dreadful appeal of innocence, but there was not innocence; you had to go back a long way further before you got innocence; innocence was a slobbering mouth, a toothless gum pulling at the teats; perhaps not even that; innocence was the ugly cry of birth.[15]

At Nelson Place, where Rose's parents live, the front door's pane is broken; the passage stinks like a lavatory'; the staircase is carpeted with old newspapers reporting rape and murder; the parents, sitting amid unwashed dishes by an unlighted stove, agree to the marriage—at a price. Effectively, Rose is sold to Pinkie for fifteen guineas. (Judas required thirty pieces of silver for his act of betrayal.) This novel's title refers not only to the sticks of rock at the site of Hale's death but also, by a conceited simile, to a human nature. Ida Arnold Says to Rose:

> Look at me. I've never changed. It's like those sticks of rock: bite it all the way down, you'll still read Brighton. That's human nature.'...
> 'Confession...Repentance,' Rose whispered.
> 'That's just religion,' the woman said. 'Believe me. It's the world we got to deal with.[16]

Human nature in Ida's view is tainted with original sin, according to the Catholic view. Confession and repentance may briefly cleanse that taint but the world at large, the corruption remains.

Like many writers from earlier times, Greene is deeply interested in what could be called metaphysical questions-about the real nature and purpose of the world, about the nature of existence even of God, about man's freedom by his own efforts to alter his circumstances or lack of freedom. Greene depicts characters who are not all complex, but who hold, profoundly in the case of Pinkie, radically different views on the matters of religion. Dallow, like Ida, sees only the immediate material world before him as do the punters who see Brighton's Jelly facade of gaiety, but not the squalor behind this. Initially Pinkie believes in a world of unseen and eternal spiritual realities and believes these to await him after death, and he aspires to better his status in this world, but he comes gradually to what Prewitt; his bent lawyer, articulates for him that 'this (this world, generally; for Pinkie Brighton) is hell; nor are we out of it.'[17] Brighton in its two aspects becomes a metaphor for heaven and hell. In this novel, in Hale's funeral service and Ida's superstitious dabbling in the 'spirit world' Pinkie ridicules the then fashionable compromise between faith and so-called 'rationalism'. Pinkie's rebuke to Dallow's 'I don't believe in what my eyes don't see. (They don't see much then')[18], could reasonably be read as the author's gibe against the blindness of the modern materialist outlook to eternal realities.

> Hale Knew before he had been in Brighton three hours that they meant to murder him[19]

This powerful and sinister sentence is the opening of *Brighton Rock* and the start of the gripping thriller. We plunge straight into danger, the underworld of suspense and fear as Elizabeth Bowen calls it while praising the opening of the novel for its wonderful scene setting. The two opposing characters in the 'Good verses Evil' struggle are Pinkie and Ida. In summary, Ida is confident, irreligious but determined to do what is right while Pinkie the catholic, is determined to be damned. Rose represents a good which completes Pinkie's evils in contrast to Ida who represents good fighting evil. She is in many ways the link between the two and a connection between good and evil.

The early novels of Graham Greene reflect certain important aspect of contemporary life. What one confronts in life today is a tragic alienation and dehumanization of man who is living in a poisoned cultural milieu. In spite of all he has achieved by way of civilization he always suffers from a sense of rootlessness, lack of purpose and insignificance as a result of the collapse of the Utopian world. The themes of alienation and anxiety, which appeared in Greene's early novels, receive more emphatic treatment in his *Brighton Rock.* The novel offers an interesting picture of the crisis of western civilization. Greene is acquainted with the rational outlook of our time which suggests that economic and environmental factors determine the behavior of the individual. Ida Arnold observes, 'Man is made by the places in which he lives.'[20] Pinkie is seized with a bitter feeling of nausea to remember his indifferent parents and the ugly environment of his early childhood and thinks that he is what his parents have made him. Pinkie complains against his childhood, 'hell lay about him in his infancy.[21] The theme of basic confrontation of the two level, of existence, the spiritual and the earthly, that the novel presents most clearly, seems to have a close affinity with the theme of different levels of conscience. Rose who understands that she and Pinkie are of the realm of good and evil and are on a different level with values different from those of the world of right and wrong which Ida and all the others inhabit, articulates the basic confrontation.

> It is her. Asking questions, soft as butter what does she know about us? She does not know that a moral sin is Right and Wrong. That is what she talks about.[22]

The experience of angst that is a characteristic aspect of modern temperament is a prominent theme of the novel. Pinkie's friends-Cubit, Spicer and Dallow-are loyal to the gang and are unaware of having a self. They are immediate men who do not recognize themselves and who are merely concerned with earning their livelihood. Ida too is a slave to the traditional ideal of justice and is ignorant of any despair of not having a self. Mr. Colleoni, a rich business man, is lost in the superficial glamour of life and Pinkie longs for peace but there is no peace for him:

> Heaven is just a word and he cannot believe in its peace: Hell was something he could trust. A brain was only capable of what it could conceive and it could not conceive what it had never experienced.[23]

Life is ugly and painful, it is

> hell and no one is out of it: "life is full of confusions, contradictions and congruities. It is ambiguous and incalculable. Pinkie sees life as a series of complicated tactical exercised as complicated as the alignments at Waterloo.[24]

As mentioned in the first chapter some apocalyptic writers start and end their novels in despair while others start them with despair and end on a note of hope. Graham

Greene is one among the latter. Hence, in spite of all nihilism in modem literature, hope of faith springing from the courage of despair, constitutes the distinguishing mark of the modern hero. Rose does not abandon hope for the future. It is enough that she loves: 'It didn't matter; she love him; she had her responsibility.'[25] Her responsibility in love is the basis of her willingness to suffer damnation with Pinkie. This forms the nucleus of the novel, its fundamental affirmation. During the final death ride, Rose is torn between her loyalty to pledge and her conscience that reminds her of her autonomous existence and she trembles inside but loses trust in herself. Towards the end of his life, Pinkie is filled with a terrible feeling of resentment for not having his chance and seeing 'his glimpse of heaven if it was only a crack between the Brighton Walls.[26] But be resists the glimpses of heaven getting to him through Rose with concentrated hatred and fear bred from the pain and treachery and squalor of his life and asserts his individuality. Though no longer a legal witness to his crime, Rose is a witness to his inwardness and even her humility seems to be a trap on him. Her boundless love, unshaken by the knowledge of his evil, is a terrible shock to him. He plans to eliminate her but tormented by anxiety, Pinkie falls a victim to despair and involves himself in a process of self-destruction.

Graham Greene protests against the perversion of Christianity by Christian institutions and refuses the ministration of the church. Though a Roman Catholic, Rose commits the mortal sin by marrying without sacraments. The idea of hell does not deter her: 'If they damn him, they have got to damn her too'.[27] She watches the people coming back from Mass and feels no envy with them: 'they had their salvation and she has Pinkie of damnation'.[28] With the possibilities of hope for the change of Pinkie exhausted, her impulses of the catholic training urge her to recant by an axiom as an alternative to existential commitment 'you can plead for him at the throne of grace'.[29] But she does not allow self deception to buttress her passion to survive. It is death not damnation that scares her. Like Rose, Pinkie too is full of hatred for the sacraments. Though he feels a faint nostalgia for the tiny dark confessional box'[30], something he has lost or forgotten or rejected, hearing the faint call of God rising from the depth of his conscience, he is not ready for confession, pinnacle and the sacrament as all this will be an awful distraction. Unable to bear the presence of existence here and now, Pinkie kills himself and, thus, commits the most serious crime to a Roman catholic who believes in hell and its fire. His death destroying his existence here now speaks of the significance of the worldly life. Rose's relation to Pinkie and her choice of life without hope and of world without end for the child, who is within her, speak of the importance of human suffering in this world.

The Power and the Glory exemplifies once again Greene's obsessional interest in the operation of evil in man's life. This novel like its predecessor, *Brighton Rock,* criticizes the dehumanizing elements in modern life and points out the irrelevance of the doctrines and ceremonies of the conventional church. Greene is critical of the modern narrowly rationalistic belief, in social Utopia. The strength of the present novel is based on an interesting contrast between the materialistic and the spiritual approach to life. The lieutenant is a staunch rationalist, who holds a purely materialistic view of life and is fanatically opposed to the church for its insistence on the unimportance of human lot in this world. He is the direct opponent of the priest as Ida is Pinkie's having no taste for music, art and religion, the lieutenant lives in a room 'as comfortless as a prison or a monastic cell.'[31] he is firmly determined to wipe out everything; to destroy everything-to be alone without any memories at all. A modern Prometheus, with a devotion only to the reality of the here and now, he is in result against pain, misery and oppression of the people and wants to drive out everything that brings misery, poverty, superstition and corruption. His mission is to create happiness for his people, to give them the whole world and he will achieve this by any means even by a massacre:

> They deserved nothing less than the truth in vacant universe mid a cooling world, the right to be happy in any way they chose. He was quite prepared lo make it massacre for their saries. He wanted to begin the world again with them, in a desert.[32]

To the lieutenant there is nothing unique or mysterious about human existence and human beings have only material needs. His ideal is a well-fed and well-clad but soul-less person. But at the novel's close when he has arrested the whisky priest, he seems to be shaken by the faith of the priest and feels lost of it as if life has drained out of the world. The imagery and the characters of the novel offer a telling picture of the hopeless mess the contemporary life is in. Stripped of family, home and country man today is drifting from place to place in search of livelihood. A victim to the complexity of modern life, he has lost the capacity to discriminate between the merely superfluous and the really indispensable. Man's preoccupation with money has become so extremely dictatorial that it prevents him from thinking about the higher goals of living and attending to the higher business of finding his soul. The novel is set in a fever stricken Mexican State a land of heat, vulture and swamp:

> ... the swamp and vultures and no children anywhere except a few in the village with belief swollen by worms who ate dust from the bank, inhumanly". "Heat", "Vultures", "decaying teeth- are symbols. "Heat" signifies restlessness and anxiety that man feels today, "vultures" are the symbols of human monstrosity and greed and "decaying teeth" stand for the stinking decay of civilization.[33]

Setting is always important and constitutive in Graham Greene, but in *The Power and the Glory* even more than elsewhere. The theme is indivisibly priest-and-land, his journey through a country whose condition, simply by being what he is, he makes a charge. The land is given to a huge abandonment; it rolls through time 'like a burning and abandoned ship.'[34] Variations on these phrases echo throughout the book. It is a landscape of terror and lust. Here the echoes are even more insistent: this is a world of treachery, violence and lust, this is the land of the corrupt and cowardly Jefe, of the fang-toothed Judas. This society is clearly our society, allegorically heightened: 'This place [the prison] was very like the world: overcrowded with lust and crime and unhappy love; it stank to Heaven...'[35] This is our world, as it presents itself to Graham Greene: corrupt but denying sin; man-centred but still in the presence of God. The primary characteristics of Greene's view of the world are unhappiness and sin; it is 'stinking to heaven,' the priest repeats, and later, 'the world's unhappy whether you're rich or poor.'[36] Seedy settings attract because one sees life as it really is, with none of the thin platforms over the abyss which normal social life constructs. Speaking in *The Lost Childhood* of the blitzed cities, Greene says:

> That, I think, is why one feels at home in London or in Liverpool or Bristol...because life there is what it ought to be.[37]

Greene's vision of the world is intensely dramatic-it alternates between the rubbish tip at the far end of the town and the outer stars, between Father Jose the apostate priest, standing in his nightshirt in his miserable compound, laughed at by the boys and called forth by his gross wife, and the galaxies towards which his hands ineffectually gesture. Hell is certainly pictured with a certain intimacy, with more intimacy than heaven, than the instances of goodness and love. They are included, are recognized intellectually, but do not seem to be felt anywhere near as strongly as the wickedness. Indeed, Greene sometimes finds only sinfulness where many of us would find something less reprehensible Mr. Tench, a morose expatriate English dentist, is a typical figure of decay. Without memory and without hope, he is making a base living out of the decay he cannot prevent. Cut off from his wife and children, he pursues the ugly profession of a dentist in the unhealthy climate and the hopeless condition of life unbearably painful. His greed for money has petrified his heart and the heat and shoddiness have drained away all initiatives. Mr. Tench is gripped with an awful sense of nausea and longs to escape, but there is no escape for him. He envies the priest: you are lucky, you can get out. Captian Fellows, the English planter, is another rootless man living in exile for a job. Cut off from the whole world, he and his wife long to keep themselves aloof from the local politics because they think that they are foreigners and have no business interfering with politics. Suffering from headache in the foreign land unsuited for health, Mrs. Fellows complains 'A cookan heat you know it will kill me to stay'[38] and insists on going back to their place. The Fellows face the vacuum created by the death of their daughter Coral-a precocious girl, receiving the right kind of education from her mother, living in the adult world in full ignorance of the word "play" and looking after all the household affairs. She is the product of a topsy-turvy state of affairs in which the distinction between childhood and adulthood is blurred and a child is made to face the responsibilities of adult life much more than he is prepared for. The result is disastrous. Hardy's Father Time, kills his brothers and sisters and then commits suicide. Greene's Coral Fellows without the ghastly morbidity of Father Time, meets a similar end. She quietly and mysteriously vanishes from the scene. Whether she also commits suicide as a result of pregnancy or some other change, is an open question. But she illustrates the disastrous effects of the modem mechanical civilization on the innocence of childhood.

Padre Jose, the old, fat and ugly priest, is another inhabitant of this shabby land. Giving up his faith, he has married in obedience to law that all priests should marry.

He has no sense of self respect and though mocked and taunted both in his home and outside, his only concern is to earn a livelihood. As the habit of self analysis enables him to see himself as he is-'fat and ugly and old and humiliated'[39]-he is in the grip of the unforgivable sin, despair unwilling to get out of this state of despair, he asks the priest, Go... go. I don't want martyrs here. I don't belong any more- Leave me alone. I'm all right as I am.'[40] Lost in the trivialities of life, Padre Jose tries to be another self. The Half-Caste, 'with two fang-like teeth jutting out over his lip'[41], exemplifies serpentine slipperiness and treachery. Pretending to be an honest Christian eager to help the priest, he is always planning to trap him. Even finally, he does succeed and he gets the reward. However, he does not seem to feel any compunction or repentance. These characters truly represent the modern man, engrossed with the material, forgetting the world of the spirit. Superficiality and loss of contact with the world of human emotions characterize man's life in our time. Against a background of these men represent various forms of loneliness and isolation, Greene sets the story of the hunted priest, his pursuit and capture.

Like Pinkie, the whisky priest is an angst-ridden character. His anxiety arises from an awareness of isolation and from the feeling that he has fallen far short of the glory of God. He fears that he can do nothing to redeem himself. He is the last priest, because the others have either fled or confirmed themselves to the law or they have been persecuted and hunted down by the police. In his present condition as an outcast and a sinner, the priest is a *parody of* a true, official priest as the abandoned wounded bitch gnawing a piece of bone in the deserted banana station of Captain Fellows is 'the parody of a watch dog.[42] Exhausted and abandoned he guards, like the bitch, his last possession i.e., faith. But the bitch retains hope; it knows no despair. The priest, on the other hand, is troubled by a sense of sharp contrast between what he was before and his present state. Now shaken by a sense of his own worthlessness, the priest prays to God to send a more worthy man to carry on the mission he has taken upon himself.

> Oh, God, send them someone more worth while to suffer for. It seemed to him a damnable mockery that they should sacrifice themselves for a whisky priest with a bastard-child.[43]

Being the last priest, he takes upon himself, at the risk of his life, the task of carrying God to the people. During the perilous journey he performs through the mountains and forests, he encounters people who signify some important aspects of the human condition and gives him a better understanding of himself and life. In the state of corruption he learns to love the poor and the unhappy and identifies himself with the common men-sinners and criminals. In the wretched prison cell he has a feeling of communion with his fellow prisoners. Touched by an extraordinary affection, he feels that he is just 'one criminal among a herd of criminals'[44] and becomes aware that the world is like a prison 'overcrowded with lust and crime and unhappy love.'[45]

The priest liberates himself from the haunting fear of death and despair and realizes the true meaning of love or of the motto equating God with love. Safe across the border in the neighboring state, the priest is moved by a sense of duty and walks back into the trap laid for him. He lays down his life for God and his beloved and accomplishes the greatest acts of love. According to the orthodox doctrine the priest dies in a state of mortal sin, but he does not fear damnation. Even the fear of pain remains in the background. The Whisky-priest can be called a real apocalyptic hero since he wants to restore order and establish utopia in the anarchic state of Mexico

The novel hints at Greene's dissatisfaction with the form, of organized religion. Formalistic religion suspends one's imagination, its piety is soulless. In her lack of love and sympathy, the pious, unimaginative woman, who is outraged by the screams of pleasure coming from a man and a woman copulating at the far end of the dark cell, exemplifies the death of the spirit. Her figure deepens this meaning more substantially when the priest finds her sleeping with 'her prim mouth open, showing strong teeth like tombs.'[46] His own past is mirrored back to him-a similar figure, not an agent of God but of death.

Because of the disgust felt by him about the evil and corruption prevailing in modem civilized countries of Europe and America, Greene prefers the primitive societies of—like Liberia and Congo, and presents them with a more loving concern in novels like *The Heart of the Matter* and *A Burnt Out Case.* These societies symbolize for him the childhood of human race uncorrupted by the touch of modem civilization which is like the adult world of experience. As Marie Beatrice Mesnet points out 'The shape of Africa, the heart of darkness, corresponds also to a state of lawlessness in a no man's land on a restless border.'[47]

Fascinated by this primitive world of Africa, Greene paid a visit to Liberia in West Africa in 1934 and toured the interior parts of the country where he came across seediness, squalor, barbarity and corruption everywhere. Greene made another journey of Africa in 1941 and lived in Sierra Leone for more than a year in connection with his official work with the British Foreign Office. His opinion about the people of Africa was slightly modified by his second visit, and he came to appreciate the backwardness of Africa and its people better than he was able to do during his first visit in 1934. Both these visits, with an interval of about seven years between them, can be said to be very significant because they have revealed Greene's interest in Africa and provided him with the setting and background for one of his greatest novels, *The Heart of the Matter*. Thus, West Africa forms the setting and background of the novel. The evil, corruption, cruelty, smuggling, deception, blackmailing and other ills amid which the hero, Scobie finds himself there, are symptomic of the general atmosphere of the seedy world that Greene seeks to present in the novel. In Africa, human nature exists in its raw unsophisticated form because here, as Scobie remarks, it 'hasn't had time to disguise itself.'[48] The situation and conditions in this world stand in sharp contrast to those of the world hereafter that hold attraction for the Catholic characters. According to Scobie, 'Heaven remained rigidly in its proper place on the other side of death, and on this side flourished the injustices, the cruelties, the meannesses, that elsewhere people so cleverly hushed up.'[49]

Scobie has been living in this world of violence, treachery, smuggling and deception for about 15 years as a police officer in Freetown (Sierra Leone). Neither he nor his wife Louise likes this world; they want some sort of escape from it. But escape is simply not possible. Louise tries to find an escape by going to South Africa for a change. But Scobie cannot find an escape from this world. Nor can he find an escape from his loveless married life with Louise, because of his Catholic faith which prohibits divorce. He has an adulterous affair with Helen, but that too does not provide to him an escape from the seedy world around him or from his disgusting wife. He is trapped by the treacherous Yusuf, and made to indulge in smuggling. The escape now lies only through suicide which is, according to his faith, a mortal sin. As Marie Beatrice Mesnet remarks:

> The world is the prison where we are held captive. War is the inevitable end called for by this corruption, and while it has not reached yet the gaudy shore of Brighton, it has left wounds still bleeding in the Mexico of *The Power and the Glory,* it is actually raging in *The Heart of the Matter.* But only through hell are we brought to Faith and Heaven. When the enemy is disclosed, one is not so easily deceived.[50]

She has also given a fine description of the setting and background of *The Heart of the Matter* in the words that follow:

> The setting of *The Heart of the Matter,* like that of *The Power and Glory* is based on personal experience originally recorded in travel book; but in this case there is a twelve years' gap between the publication of *Journey Without Maps* in 1936 and the novel in 1948, and in the interval Greene had spent a year in Freetown during 1942 and 1943. It is to this visit that the story of Scobie can be traced back. Greene had made several attempts in 1936 to turn his African experiences into fiction. In *The Heart of the Matter* he seems at last to have succeeded in delivering himself of the long contemplated theme of Africa, and more specifically the Coast, that ruin of land not so far from the central darkness. The geographical and historical background of the novel is derived from the author's contact with the squalor of the unhappiness and the involuntary injustices of tired men and from the experience of inertia gained there, where worms of malaria, even without yellow fever, are enough to cloud life...there is little genuine primitiveness in the cosmopolitan world of the ruled. The natives have been spoilt by the seedy civilization introduced by the British. They are Creoles and not the real niggers as in the Protectorate. They try to initiate the civilization of white men, who are afraid of them. It is with this corrupt people that Scobie has to deal.[51]

The British colony of Freetown in Sierra Leone is a microcosm of the seedy world which Greene frequently depicts in his novels. In this colony, Scobie finds himself in a strange predicament. He finds it to be a place abounding in evil and corruption.

> There was a retort in this colony to every accusation. There was always a blacker corruption elsewhere to be pointed at. The scandal mongers of the secretariat fulfilled a useful purpose-they kept alive the idea that no one was to be trusted.[52]

Against the setting and background of this ugly, sinful and corrupt world is played the drama of the conflict between Good and Evil, Sin and Sainthood, and Salvation and Damnation, in this novel. The world of the novel is dark and dismal, but it is often illumined by the light of love, faith, pity and God's mercy. *The Heart of the Matter* is set in a West African coastal town which, like Brighton and Mexico, is a picture of hell, a province of "Greenland". The details of the British colony are based on Greene's actual experience during his stay in Sierra Leone during the years 1941 and 1943. The filth of weather and extremely hot climate all suited for the growth of the ugly fauna, rats, cockroaches, flies and mosquitoes harbouring pestilential diseases and convicting the earth into a hell. The imagery derived from the descriptions of natural objects evokes the actual milieu of treachery, violence and lust. The lizard on the wall hunting, 'for moths and cockroaches' 'the rusty hand cuffs' and 'the broken rosary'[53] all convey a picture of ugliness and decay much similar to *The Power and the Glory* which is punctuated by the sound of vultures flapping their wings on corrugated iron roofs. *The Heart of the Matter* is full of references to the continual sights of rats and cockroaches. Greene's carrion birds and beasts are normally conventional symbols of the corruption and horror of a world without God. The natives, Syrians as well as Europeans, are all swallowed up in corruption. The odour of human meanness and injustice pervades the entire world. People realize their selfish ends by having recourse to lies, evasions and bribes. Syrians run all the stores in the country and indulge in diamond smuggling which the Government has failed to control. Yusuf, a shameless Villain, is a typical representative of this world. He is a smuggler who 'sells bad liquor, hoards cottons against a French invasion, and seduces the nursing sisters from the military hospital.'[54]

Scobie, a just, honest and incorruptible police officer, though the promotion is commissionership, which is due, is denied to him, chooses to live in this cheap, vulgar place fit for meanness, malice and snobbery. Scobie's decision to live in a place whose moral and natural conditions are unfit for decent living, is a sign of protest against the evils of a corrupt urban society, seedy meretricious. Scobie's love for simple African life is reflected in the following lines:

> Nobody here could ever talk about a heaven on earth. Heaven remained rigidly in its proper place on the other side of the death and on this side flourished the injustices, the cruelties, the meanness that elsewhere people so cleverly hushed up. Here you could love human beings nearly as God loved them, knowing the worst. You didn't love a pose, a pretty dress, a sentiment artfully assumed.[55]

Scobie's suicide, the unforgivable sin to a catholic, is a sign of protest against dogma. Scobie is torn by a conflict of loyalty either to his religion or to his innate humanism. He betrays his government and violates the rules of his church with his eyes open and knowing the consequences. The shedding off his loyalties to the norms supplied by the external forces and acting in sincerity to his own self point to Greene's protest against conventional standards of morality, social as well as religious. What matters to Greene is pure human love rather than traditional God or Religion. He writes out of human sympathy and understanding and his writing is haunted by the paradox of the innocence of the criminal and the guilt of the faultless. Greene admits in an interview that one of the things which interests him most is discovering humanity in the apparently inhuman character.

The End of the Affair, like Greene's other religious novels is mainly concerned with his leaning towards the force of the 'irrational, man's sickening despair effecting with the church and its dogma. Greene's apocalyptic vision lies in his partial despiritualisation of modern life which is best understood in terms of the gradual evaporation of our period of authentic 'paradigmatic experience.'[56]

Henry, an important assistant secretary in the ministry of pensions, is the typical product of present abstract and calculated systems. As he has come under the possessions of complex social machinery, he is completely shut from himself. His pre-occupation with office work has deprived him of his humanity and he has since long, ceased to feel any physical desire for Sarah and needs her simply for companionship. Worried and full of despair, Henry is living in terrible insecurity because he feels excluded from Sarah's coincidence and is afraid of being condemned to a life of terrible loneliness and barren solitude. Both Sarah and Bendrix are in the pleasures of the moment. Sarah, a woman of loose morals whose husband is sexually impotent, has illicit relationship with different kinds of men-and Bendrix is only one of many men-the favorite lover for the moment. A woman without scruples, impervious to the passage of time, she is concerned with 'the pleasurable present and commits adultery in her husband's house, remorselessly and not haunted by guilt.'[57] As she does not believe in God remorse dies with the act. Like Sarah, Bendrix, a middle-aged novelist, sensual, sophisticated and agnostic, too is living the aesthetic way of life and to him only the moment matters. He is very methodical and does his quota of work-'Daily five hundred words.'[58] Nothing, not even a love affair, can upset his self imposed discipline and alter his schedule. He is not interested in anything else in the world except for his writing. At the ethical level, both Sarah and Bendrix suffer from a terrible feeling of anxiety and despair. Sarah's prayer, 'let him be alive, and I will believe...I will give him up forever, only let him be alive.'[59]

Gripped with the absurd dread of the unknown and the feeling of loneliness, emptiness and desolation, Sarah longs to believe 'in some kind of a God, something vague, amorphous, cosmic... stretching out of the vague into the concrete human life, like a powerful vapour and to become part of that vapor' and escape the seriousness and uncertainty of choice. But she can't invent a belief. The feelings of misery and emptiness make her rebellious and desperate and like Scobie, she questions the existence of a merciful God: 'he does not exist...He can't exist You can't have a merciful God & his despair.'[60]

Failing to invent belief in God, Sarah tries out her methods to escape self-hood, but there's no escape. She tries to convince herself that a vow to someone she does not believe in is not all that important and has recourse to sex and drink to avoid the implication of her vow. But, it doesn't work. There is no joy left in her life; there is no lust for Bendrix either. She can't escape feeling despair. The fanaticism of the rationalist preacher Richard Smythe with livid spots on his left cheek, who she visits, hoping that he will convince her to break her bargain, 'gives her a sense of inverted belief[61] and fixes 'the superstition deeper'.[62] Sarah's desire to believe in absolutes and abstractions and love Bendrix without seeing him proves to be a desperate cry. She cannot believe in anything but her own experience: 'Even a God can't love something that does not exist he cannot love something he cannot see'[63]

Thus Sarah's efforts to dispel despair result in its reduplication. Like Sarah, Bendrix too suffers from a deep sense of despair resulting from the frustration of his desire. Shocked by the hidden end of his love affair with Sarah and the vision of her abandoning herself to another man. Bendrix, like Scobie, plans his suicide saving his sleeping pills and is prevented by the memory of the look of disappointment of Sarah's face. He is filled with revolt against God when his hope to win Sarah from his intangible divine adversary 'imprisoned behind the altar'[64] is frustrated and is condemned to a crippled existence, 'the empty life, odorless, antiseptic, the life of a prison.'[65] Bendrix's hatred for God is the reflection of his own tormented mind like Lear cursing the dements. In spite of his combat with his rival and firm determination not to surrender himself to him he is afraid that his hatred may turn into belief which will be a triumph for God.

Bendrix thinks that 'hatred seems to operate the same glands as love, it even produces the same actions.'[66] Bendrix is full of hatred for God who remains the tempter and destroyer of human happiness till the end:

> You are a devil God, tempting us to leap. With your great schemes. You ruin our happiness like a harvester ruins a mouse's nest. I hate you God, I hate you as though you existed.[67]

Bendrix's anxiety about his situation implies anxiety about human situation. Like a natural man, he experiences the absurd in life and sees God as a corruptor of human happiness. Unable to outlive the tension created in her by the conflict between her faith and her overwhelming 'ordinary corrupt human love.' And touched by universal suffering, she prays to God for death:

> I don't know how I am going to live in this pain and longing and I'm praying to god all the time that he won't be hard on me, that he won t keep me alive.[69]

Though she does not kill herself like Scobie, her dying of uncared pneumonia comes very close to self slaughter. Bendrix's prayer at the close of the novel to leave him 'alone forever'[70] in a state of anxiety ridden impatience is suggestive of rational leap to faith. The prayer calls to mind Job in the midst of his suffering:-

> 'Are not the days of my life few? Let me alone, that I may find a little comfort....'[71]

In A *Burnt out Case (1961),* Greene focuses more emphatically on the themes of suffering and crisis. The burnt-out quality present throughout the novel is in fact a telling embodiment of the state of mind and feeling or absence of feeling that Greene is seeking to convey. The characters' argument about God's existence and nature take place in a context which is both a test of belief and a justification for unbelief for, as we are unobtrusively reminded, they frequently occur within sight of monstrous human suffering. A passage, quite early in the book, demonstrates compassion with neither sentimentality nor Voyeurism:

> The air in the hospital lay heavily and sweetly upon them: it was never moved by a fan or a breeze. Querry was conscious of the squalor of the bedding-cleanliness was not important to the leper, only to the healthy. The patients brought their own mattresses which they had probably possessed for a lifetime rough sacking from which the straw like ill wrapped packages of meat. On the Veranda the walking cases sat out of the sun-if you could call a walking case a man who, when he moved, had to support his huge swollen testicles with both hands. A woman with palsied eyelids who could not close her eyes or even blink sat in a patch of shade out of the merciless light. A man without fingers nursed a baby on his knee, and another man lay flat on the Veranda with one breast long and drooping and tested like a woman's.[72]

However, strong allegorical emphasis of *A Burnt-Out Case* and its meaning are finally worked through in the life of a central personality-Querry. Querry detests laughter like a bad smell and is, in fact, physically incapable of laughing or even smiling. His capacity for feeling is frozen. Towards the end of the book, Querry remarks to Dr.Colin:

> 'I suffer, therefore I am.' I wrote something like that once in my diary, but I can't remember what or when, and the word was not suffer. What he did write, in the novel's first sentence, was a parody of Descartes which means that I feel discomfort, therefore I am alive. Discomfort is entirely personal, of course; an itch, an ache, a bad smell are powerful reminders of the self, capable of distracting us from the beauty of art, nature, another person. Suffering, on the other hand, can hardly be entirely egotistical.[73]

However, self-pitying we may be, suffering brings us inescapably into relation with others, either in what is done to us or in what we do. Querry believes that his mind and spiritual mutilation has gone so far that suffering is impossible for him and asks Dr. Colin to teach him how to suffer because 'I only know the mosquito bites.'[74] Again, this is an echo from something much earlier when the superior of a mission had remarked, in response to Querry's admission of emotional deadness, 'Oh. Well, you know, suffering is something which will always be provided when it is required.'[75]

Querry learns to feel suffering again through the awakening of his personal interest in Deo Gratias as well as in the general plight of the lepers. Paradoxically, Querry finds suffering through the peace of the mission. The atheist Dr. Colin and Catholic priests are united in one thing, their overriding involvement in bettering of the leper's existence. In an exchange of letter, with Evelyn Waugh recorded in *Ways of Escape,* Greene says:

> With a writer of your genius and insight I certainly would not attempt to hide behind the time-old gag that an author can never be identified with his characters. Of course in some of Querry's reactions there are reactions of mine, just as in some of Fowler's reactions in *The Quiet American* there are reactions of mine...Fowler, I hope, was a more jealous man than I am, and Querry, I fear, was a better man than I am, I wanted to give expression to various states or modes of belief and unbelief.[76]

From the above quote, we get to know that Greene returned to the central question of faith and belief only in *A Burnt-Out Case* (1961). Set in a Catholic leprosarium in the Congo and owing much to Conrad's *The Heart of Darkness,* the novel tells the story of Querry, a world-famous Catholic architect who has lost all belief in God. He is the metaphorical leper, deadened to desire and love, as well as in psychological pain. In the growing relationship with his servant, a leper named Deo Gratias, and in his interactions with both, the committed atheist Doctor Collins and the priests who staff the leprosarium, Querry is slowly cured of his despair and isolation. Yet the protagonist's new orientation toward faith in God is left ambiguous, for the novel ends with this murder at the hands of Rycker, a jealous husband who wrongly suspects Querry of impregnating his wife. Like many of Greene's previous texts, it is left up to those who survive to pronounce possible conclusions about belief. In the final dialogue that closes the novel, the atheist doctor maintains that Querry had learned merely a kind of fidelity in serving others.

The novel's investigation into the failure of religious belief to sustain the Catholic protagonist, Querry, was so pronounced that Evelyn Waugh personally wrote to Greene that he saw the book as a recantation of faith. Greene responded to Waugh:

> I wanted to give expression to various states or moods of belief and unbelief. The doctor.. .represents a settled and easy atheism: the father superior a settled and easy belief: Father Thorn an unsettled form of belief and Querry an unsettled form of disbelief.[77]

In later remarks about the inspiration for writing the book, Greene clarified his position:

> Evelyn Waugh and I inhabited different wastelands. I find nothing unsympathetic in atheism, even in Marxist atheism. My I wasteland is inhabited by the pious "suburbans" of whom I had too carelessly written—I had not meant the piety of simple, who accept God without question, but the piety of the educated, the established, who seem to own their Roman Catholic image of God, who have ceased to look for him because they considered they have found him.[78]

Waugh was not alone in his attempt at diagnosing

Greene's health, for many of the reviews and critical essays read the novel as an indication of Greene's burnt out faith.

The protagonist is "Burnt" by his too easily accommodated belief system and the institution that supports it. Querry represents Greene's attempt to expose the difficult quest for authentic religious faith. *A Burnt-Out Case* presents the theme of man's alienation in the present century, his feeling of anxiety and emptiness of life. The novel emphasizes Greene's usual criticism of modern life that has deprived man of his existential humanity, his love for the simple and peaceful life of the African natives that is still capable of revitalizing man. The novel offers an interesting contrast between contemporary civilized life and the primitive African life. The pressures of society exerted largely through the press mould the lives of the people in stereotyped ways and produce a world of conformists. In such a world the very possibility of choice and decision is taken away. The decisions have already been taken for us and all we are expected to do is to conform to them and to reinforce them. As a consequence, the modern man is a slave to public opinion and he submits to having all his thinking response and living done for him for others. He has become too enervated to think, respond and act by his own capacity. As he is circumscribed, a natural and spontaneous behaviour on his part is impossible. He is what Heidegger calls "das man", a man lost in the crowd. Instead of living independently and obeying his inner self, he lives the crowd life. The pressure of the ordered systematized life has made man selfish, brutal and violent whereas in the primitive way of life man is still a matter of concern for his fellow beings. Greene criticizes the dehumanizing elements of modern life, condemns all political and economic progress and reveals a nostalgic longing for more human and personal conditions of life. Through Querry, a world famous architect, Greene offers a horrifying picture of a man who is sick of European civilization. Bored of his worldly success, Querry tries to escape to a remote leper colony. Driven by a sense of revulsion, he, like Conrad's Jim, wants to be in a place where nothing will remind him of his past.

Querry's flight into the heart of darkness, a leproserie deep in the Congo, is a sign of revolt against modem life. Nauseated by the contemporary disorders, Querry seeks refuge in the so-called dark world. His inward hollowness-'Nothing, I want nothing. I suffer nothing'[79]-is the symbol of the spiritual hollowness of the contemporary materialistic civilization. He represents the bewildered failure of feeling and imagination of our terrible world. The suffering of the world's untouchables, the humanity of Doctor Colin and the priests, the peaceful life of the leproserie stir a sense of kinship with the people in distress and revive his love for man. The representative of the civilized world, on the other hand, which Querry has left behind, stands as hurdles in the way of his self-knowledge. Rycker, the manager of a palm-oil plantation, a smug pious, formalistic, self-centered catholic, is a dehumanized figure. A man interested in moral theology, he bores his young wife with his spiritual discussion. He is proud, full of self-importance and has no genuine sympathy for the lepers. He helps the mission only out of charity. Rycker propagates Querry's presence in the colony and puts in his way Parkinson, a vulgar, corrupt, English journalist, so as to obstruct Querry's self-knowledge. With the arrival of Parkinson, the great world, which Querry has left, makes a path to his door and Querry's quest for identity is interrupted by the sensational and ridiculous accounts of his achievement spread by the journalist. The doppelganger motive suggested in the relationship between the Whisky-priest and the Half-caste and between Scobie and Yusef is hinted at here. As Jim finds his own reflection in gentleman Brown, Querry feels that Parkinson is a looking glass which returns such a straight image. Writing articles entitled 'An Architect of Souls', 'The Hermit of Congo', Parkinson destroys Querry's dream of 'pendele.'[80] Doctor Colin aptly reflects:

> The fools, the interesting fools, they exist everywhere... He had been cured of all but his success; but you can't cure success...Success is like that too- a mutilation of the natural man.[81]

The novel lays stress on the ethical way of existence. Doctor Collin and the priests of the mission are dedicated to the improvement of the hospital and to the welfare of the lepers. The priests are not as much interested in the rules and the conventions of the church as in the service of the patients. They are unconcerned with private lives and their tolerance encompasses even atheists and unmarried parishioners who have a baby every year from a different man. As they are interested in the welfare of the people, they are against wasting money on a Church because the people still live in mud huts. The Superior, who is more endearing and charitable than others, is a humanist to whom human love is superior to the divine love. The Superior reflects:

> I do not tell you to do good things for the love of God. That is very hard. Too hard for many of use. It is much easier to show mercy because a child weeps or to love because a girl or a young man pleases your eye.[82]

Like the priests, Doctor Colin too is only concerned with the betterment of human conditions-James Noxon has aptly remarked:

> In a merciless climate, against official parsimony and native suspicion, he works to salvage the diseased wreckage that an indifferent nature throws his way.[83]

Unlike the Fathers, he has no belief to support him in his hard vocation and one can learn from him that 'it's possible for an intelligent man to make his life without a God.'[84] Examining a three-year old leper, the Doctor says to the Superior, 'Your God-must feel a bit disappointed when he looks at this world of his.'[85] The

Superior's reply, 'God cannot feel disappointment nor pain',[86] is not convincing. The Doctor does not need a God who is capable of pain. He says, 'Perhaps that's why I don't care to believe in Him.'[87] Here one is reminded of Camus's Dr Rieux confronting the Bishop or Oran with, 'until my dying day, I shall refuse to love a scheme of things in which children all put to torture.'[88]

Dr. Rieux is unwilling to cease curing the sick and to leave that to an all-powerful God. Behind their selfless service, the chief motive of Dr. Rieux as well as of Dr.Colin is their sense of sharing human suffering. Dr Rieux says: 'There are sick people and they need caring.'[89] Living away from the modern busy civilized life, Doctor Colin and the Priests are endowed with all the laudable qualities that distinguish man from animals, while Querry, born and brought up in the city, suffer from alienation. No longer an aesthete designing a building or making love to a woman for his own solitary pleasure, inflected with the boredom of a satiated man, Querry lapses into cynical detachment from the aesthetic way of life and swings from the mood of melancholy, i.e. despair and sickness unto death. Self-love and self-expression, which were behind all he did, have destroyed everything, even his true self, because 'self-expression is a hard and selfish thing. It eats everything, even the self.'[90] Querry parallels Karenin of Tolstoy, whom life had been geared to professional ambition and who felt totally isolated in his misery. Querry's heart is burnt out and his spiritual condition resembles the physical state of a leper who though technically cured, is mutilated. Querry is aware of the loss of his identity, and self-identity is his only concern: 'I am looking after myself... He is totally vacant and feels no pity for the miserable life of the lepers. 'Human beings are not my country'[92], he writes in his journal. Like Conrad's Jim who feels 'responsible for every life in the land,'[93] Querry tries to ease his bleeding conscience by working for the people in a place where he is a stranger. He begins a slow and painful recovery of his real self amid the squalor and the suffering at the leproserie. The first sign of the string of a new life is seen when his Negro boy, Deo Gratias, has an accident and Querry goes out into the bush to rescue him. This accident gives him an odd feeling that he is needed. Gradually Querry has a twinge of suffering and begins to feel part of the human condition. The suffering of the African lepers brings about a remarkable change in Querry's heart and he begins to feel responsible for them. With the sequence of human feeling he allows himself to be persuaded to design the building or the new hospital and in this way he makes himself useful to the mission. Though his desire to reach "Pendele", the place of contentment, does not materialize, he is killed when his shriveled soul is coming to life again in a kind of resurrection. One may note a few points of compassion between Querry and Jean Tarrow of Camus's *The Plague*. Nauseated with the unjust and the meaningless world, Tarrow like Querry, retreats into a Plague stricken town, Oran. As Querry feels like a leper, Tarrow has plague already before he comes to this town, encounters it here and is anxious to get out of it. Querry is looking for a reason for living, and finds one in being useful to the lepers; Tarrow longs for peace through serving others. He thinks he must do what he can 'to cease being plague-stricken and that is the only way in which we can hope for some peace.'[94]

Though Querry, like Greene himself finds an interest in the act of living, he is caught in a struggle between belief and unbelief. The Priest and Scobie are believers. Sarah yields to belief and Bendrix resists belief. But all these stances are merged in Querry who is always troubled by his lack of faith and keeps on 'fingering it like a sore'[95] which he wants to get rid of, as Dr. Colin puts it. Querry's soul is always in a state of restlessness because it is constantly looking for itself and does not find itself. The kind of absence of itself from itself is suggestive of the state of being on the way tending towards God. Thus the novel conveys Greene's reaction against the present industrialized civilization that has dehumanized man and his love for the simple, innocent and peaceful primitive life. Greene also reveals his close affinity with the writers like Kierkegard, Marcel, Jaspers, Baber and Tillich and like them he is also preoccupied with the boredom, vulgarity and seediness of the modern civilization in which the springs of life have dried up and man has lost his true self.

He is critical of the dehumanizing effects of the present civilization and suggests, through characters like Scobie and Henry an escape to the primitive African life, which is much superior to our civilization. Greene is deeply shocked by the initialization of modern life on account of too much emphasis on materialistic outlook. The liberal outlook that believes in social progress is undermined, as it ignores the presence of the irrational and incongruous elements in life. Greene rejects the conventional middle class values that Ida Arnold of *Brighten-Rock* and the Lieutenant of police in *The Power and the Glory* represents and insists on the significance of the authentic experience of the mysterious which has evaporated in our time as a result of scientific progress. Hostile to the right calculating rules of life in which modem scientific rationalism interested and believing in the endless possibilities of human life and limitless power of human ill. Greene emphasizes the existential character who is someone whom concrete facts of life are closer than concepts and for Henry real may not be equivalent to the intelligible. Faith is still present and wages a ceaseless war against the rational outlook, as is seen in *The Power and the Glory* and *The End of the Affair*.

Set in great London, with an epilogue set in Moscow, *The Human Factor* explores the virtue in disloyalty to and betrayal of the state secret service apparatus. Greene focuses the novel not on the public diplomacy between nations but on the ambiguous alliances of the cold war. With little explicit religious thread, the text is often expressed in elegiac terms, characters mourning a bygone era, when faith and belief might have once made a difference, a searching for a moral consensus that had once informed and analyzed the actions of institutions and governments. Yet faith and belief-whether in God or humanity-are the traces that linger on the edge of the text, implicating the post-Christian political order of both the Western powers and communist Russia. The search for a stable factor-the human factor of the title-is uneasily negotiated in a universe denied and deprived of Greene's usual recourse to explicit Catholic images and beliefs. Graham Greene through the use of the espionage genre allows for a political allegorization of his religious concerns. The political wasteland of espionage dramatizes the religious vacuum in the twentieth century political realities.

Maurice Castle is a 62-year old Englishman who is working in the British secret service and is a Russian agent. Castle had worked in South Africa years before he had fallen in love with one of his agents, a black woman named Sarah; he had married her even though she had already became pregnant by a man of her own race. Castle enlists a communist named Carson to help him get Sarah and her son, Sam, out of the country. When Sarah is deported he follows her to England, moves them into the security of a suburban home in Berkhamsted and gets himself established at the ministry of intelligence, Ml6. Out of a sense of gratitude for Carson's help, Castle agrees to be double agent for Russia, but only in African affairs. When a leak is discovered in Castle's section, his superiors attempt to quietly hunt down the culprit and secretly eliminate him before the word leaks to the press. Castle's unambitious and dull demeanor makes him appear so harmless that attention turns to his assistant, Arthur Davis, who is suspected because of his love for flashy sports cars, expensive port and penthouse magazines. The Sinister Dr.Percival is called in to help colonel Daintry, the chief of internal security, with the ongoing investigation. Percival takes matters into his own hands and gives Davis's lethal dose of an untested toxic substance in order to disguise his death as a result of liver disease. Daintry, himself an unhappy man is outraged at Percival's actions but feels helpless to do anything. Castle realizes that Davis's unfortunate end should have been his own, and he informs his contact that he is finished as a double agent. The moment of crisis, however, comes after the arrival of Castle's old enemy, Cornelius Muller, the chief of security in South Africa. Muller and his apartheid government are now working in conjunction with the British. As a sign of the detente between them, Muller gives castle some notes on operation Uncle Remus, an American programme for military operations to keep South Africa from the communists.

With Castle's pro-African sympathies-he calls himself a naturalized Black"-he makes the decision to save innocent African lives by sending a final report to Russia, even if it means blowing his cover. He sets his defection in motion, leaving behind Sarah and Sam at his mother's house with the hope of their joining him later in Moscow. In a cold apartment, Castle bides his time. After losing his temper with his Russian hosts, he gets connected on the phone to his wife who is being kept in England by the vengeful Dr. Percival, who threatens to separate Sarah from her son if she attempts to flee. On the phone, Castle tells Sarah of his hopes of their coming to Russia, but he never hears her reply- 'Maurice, Maurice, please go on hoping'- because the connection has been cut. Greene's novel ends on this pessimistic note, with the possibility of hope reduced to its narrower margins.

In the absence of actual war, the cold war becomes the ultimate power game. God has become a refugee, and belief in God seems hopeless in a world where professionals from the national intelligence agencies decide the fate of individuals. In this political climate, Greene relocates Newman's "original calamity"[96] in the actions, methods, and philosophy of security organizations, for under the guise of English manners, they empower, as well as conceal, the immorality of the political system.

Liberation theology's articulation of the systematic reality of sin is echoed in the corruption, coercion and will to power that fuel the world in which Greene situates his characters. Apartheid becomes a metaphor not only for injustice in South Africa but also for the laws and rules that isolate and perpetuate the "apartness."

The Human Factor thoroughly explores the tragic mess of contemporary life. Themes of man's deep feeling of boredom, anxiety and nausea arising from secret codes and the bureaucracy and the problem of the committed and the uncommitted in confrontation with the absurd are emphatically projected in the present novel. Greene pours scorn on the evils of the present industrialized Western civilization that has created a widespread feeling of resentment and a problem of man's self-awareness. The unclean bureaucracy, which is the characteristic of modern life, has dehumanizing influence upon the individuals and produces heartless men who can shamelessly justify even the murder of an innocent man and captives of society existing in painless obedience. There is a decrease in the level of responsibility people feel for one another and human relationships have sunk to the level of market values. Man is gripped by an anxious sense of being left alone in the midst of nothingness. Love is 'a total risk',[97] one fears to speak of others because it invited danger;

> Love and hatred are both dangerous…A man in love walks through the world like an anarchist, carrying a time bomb.[98]

The worst effect is that most people accept their conditions and become insensitive to their captivity to the system. Anyone who attempts to revolt becomes the victim of bitter resentment find the full force of institution, legal and penal, is brought to bear upon him. Most of these characters experience a moment of uneasy relation between personal and professional self. They suffer from an invisible inner panic that has nothing to do with competence and self confidence. This is the sense of incongruity that rises from the confusion between social and personal confirmation.

To conclude, it could be said that Greene's writings emanate out of this sense of loss that results from the passing of an old world-view. Of all the recent analysis of apocalypse, no one has expressed this more precisely than Amos Wilder:

> Common to the true Apocalyptic is a situation characterised by anomie, a loss of "world," or erosion of structures, psychic and cultural, with the consequent nakedness to Being or immediacy to the Mystery. Hence the rhetorics of this "panic" exposure in which existence itself is at stake, involving antimonies of life and death, light and darkness, knowledge and nescience, order and chaos. And it can never be only a question of the individual. It is a juncture which renews the archaic crisis of all existence, that of survival, the viability of life, the viability of the human. Since inherited structures and mediacies of a dependable order are forfeit, the only available dramatizations of the crisis and of any projected "future" will necessarily have a pre-cultural character. Pre-cultural, first in a temporal sense: a return to archaic motifs and to deeply buried hierophanies of the community. But pre- cultural also in the sense of a language responsive to the unmediated dynamics that underlie all Being and Becoming.[99]

What John R. May writes in his book[100] stands true to Greene's novels, that that the literary phase of apocalypse from the middle of the nineteenth century to the present, reflects a strong reaction against the easy optimism of the late nineteenth and early twentieth centuries and later a poignant response to the succession of global hot and cold wars. Greene also becomes a representative figure of the moral chaos of his age which Mircea Eliade sums up as the manifestation of the *Kali Yuga* in this way:

> It is the only age in which property alone confers social rank; wealth becomes the only motive of the virtues, passion and lust the only bonds between the married, falsehood and deception the first condition of success in life, sexuality the sole means of enjoyment, while external, merely ritualistic religion is confused with spirituality. For several thousand years, be it understood, we have been living in *Kali Yuga.*[101]

References

1. Jerry H. Bryant. *The Open decision. London*: The Free Press, 1970.
2. Northop Frye. *Anatomy of Criticism,* Princeton: Princeton Univ. Press. 1957.
3. Graham Greene. *A Sort of Life.* New York: Simon and Schuster, 1971. Pp.117-118
4. Apparently the term was coined by A.C. Marshall, who, in *Horizon* (May 1940), said that Greenland was characterized by seediness. Eventually, *A Supplement to the Oxford English Dictionary* I (1972) included the word, defmmg it thus: 'A term used to describe the world of depressed seediness reputedly typical of the setting and characters of the novels of Graham Greene.
5. Graham Greene. *Brighton Rock.* London: Heinemann, 1938, p. 261.
6. William Shakespeare. *Hamlet.* London: Cambridge University Press.
7. John Atkins. *Graham Greene.* London: Calder & Boyars, 1966, pp. 42-43
8. *Brighton Rock.* P. 23.
9. Graham Greene. *The Heart of the Matter.*
10. The image of the enemy troops fraterninizing is widespread in contemporary fiction. It recurs in *The Heart of the Matter,* is an actual event an a key experience in Malraux's Les *Noyers de l'altenberg,* and is elaborated into book length allegory in Faulkner's A *Fable.*
11. *Brighton Rock.* P. 45.

12. Cedric Watts. *A Preface to Greene*. Singapore. Pearson Education, 2003.
13. *Brighton Rock,* p. 145.
14. *Brighton Rock,* p. 45.
15. *Brighton Rock,* pp. 202-3.
16. *Brighton Rock,* p. 207.
17. *Brighton Rock,* p. 45.
18. *Brighton Rock,* p. 212.
19. *Brighton Rock,* p. 1.
20. *Brighton Rock,* p. 37.
21. *Brighton Rock,* p. 69.
22. *Brighton Rock,* p. 114.
23. *Brighton Rock,* p. 230.
24. *Brighton Rock,* p. 229.
25. *Brighton Rock,* p. 229.
26. *Brighton Rock,* p. 230.
27. *Brighton Rock,* p. 191
28. *Brighton Rock,* p. 196.
29. *Brighton Rock,* p. 249.
30. *Brighton Rock,* p. 110.
31. Graham Greene. *The Power of the Glory*. London: Heinemann, 1940, p. 24.
32. *The power of the Glory,* p. 58
33. *The power of the Glory,* p. 34.
34. *The power of the Glory,* p. 55.
35. *The power of the Glory,* p. 66.
36. *The power of the Glory,* p. 67.
37. Graham Greene. *The Lost Childhood*. London: Eyre Spottiswoode, 1951, p.55.
38. *The Power of the Glory,* p. 49.
39. *The Power of the Glory,* p. 118.
40. *The Power of the Glory,* p. 112.
41. *The Power of the Glory,* p. 42.
42. *The Power of the Glory,* p. 135.
43. *The Power of the Glory,* p. 128.
44. *The Power of the Glory,* p. 125.

45. *The Power of the Glory,* p. 133.
46. *The Power of the Glory,* p. 273.
47. Marie Beatrice Mesnet. Graham *Greene and the Heart of the Matter.* London: Cresset Press, 1954, p. 12.
48. *The Power of the Glory,* p. 36.
49. *The Power of the Glory,* p. 37.
50. Marie Beatrice Mesnet. *Graham Greene and the Heart of the Matter.* London: Cresset Press, 1954.
51. *Graham Greene and the Heart of the Matter,* pp. 22-29.
52. Graham Greene and *The Heart of the Matter,* New York: Penguin, 1984, p. 34.
53. *The Heart of the Matter,* p. 13.
54. *The Heart of the Matter,* p.67.
55. *The Heart of the Matter,* p. 35.
56. Karl Mannheism. *Diagonosis of Our time.* New York: New York University Press, 1944, p. 146.
57. Graham Greene. *The End of the Affair.* London: Heinemann. 1951, p. 50.
58. *The End of the Affair,* p. 19.
59. *The End of the Affair,* p. 95.
60. *The End of the Affair,* p. 93.
61. *The End of the Affair,* p. 115.
62. *The End of the Affair,* p. 118.
63. *The End of the Affair,* p. 101.
64. *The End of the Affair,* p. 128.
65. *The End of the Affair,* p. 145.
66. *The End of the Affair,* p. 27.
67. *The End of the Affair,* p. 191.
68. *The End of the Affair,* p. 89.
69. *The End of the Affair,* p. 146.
70. *The End of the Affair,* p. 192.
71. The Book of Job, *The Bibler.* Chapter 10.
72. Graham Greene. *A Burnt-Out Case.* London: Heinemann, 1961, p.66.
73. *A Burnt - Out Case.* P. 4.
74. *A Burnt - Out Case.* P. 1.
75. *A Burnt - Out Case.* P.2.

76. *A Burnt - Out Case*. P. 195.
77. *Ways of Escapes,* p. 263.
78. *Ways of Escapes,* p. 267.
79. *A Burnt - Out Case*. P.16.
80. *A Burnt - Out Case*. P.165.
81. *A Burnt - Out Case*. P.197.
82. *A Burnt - Out Case*. P.81.
83. James Noxon. "Kieregard's Stages & A Burnt out Case." *Review of English Literature,* 3, 1962, p.99.
84. *A Burnt - Out Case*. P.82.
85. *A Burnt - Out Case*. P.199.
86. *A Burnt - Out Case*. P.75.
87. *A Burnt - Out Case*. P.87.
88. Albert Camus. *The Plague*. London: Stuart Gilbert, 1947, p. 203.
89. *The Plague, p.* 107.
90. *A Burnt - Out Case*. P.46.
91. *A Burnt - Out Case*. P.135.
92. *A Burnt - Out Case*. P.51.
93. Joseph Conrad *Lord Jim*. London: Blackwood, 1900, P. 297.
94. *The Plague, p.* 201.
95. *A Burnt - Out Case*. P.192.
96. Interview with V.S. Prichett for the *London Times,* 18 March 1978.
97. Graham Greene. *The Human Factor*. London: Bodley Head, 1978, p. 20.
98. *The human Factor,* p. 141.
99. Amos N. Wilder. "The Rhetoric of Ancient and Modern Apocalyptic." Paper read before the American Academy of Religion, 1970.
100. John R. May. *Toward a New Earth*. London: University of Notre Dame Press, 1972, p. 19.
101. Mircea Eliade. *Images and Symbols*. New York: Sheed & Ward, 1952. p. 64.

Epilogue

The present book has attempted to situate Graham Greene in the context of the modern apocalyptic literary tradition in order to bring out certain essential aspects of Greene. The study has focused on most of his major novels to substantiate the argument that Greene's whole outlook is shaped by his realization that the world is fast approaching its catastrophic point. The book has also attempted to establish a link between all his seemingly different thematic concerns in order to realize its objective of presenting Greene as a major apocalyptic writer of the 20th century. The overriding concern has been to demonstrate that Greene's apocalyptic vision provides the key to the understanding of his fiction. Greene's preoccupation with the ideas discussed in detail in the preceding chapters reveals that more than any other major novelist of the 20th century, he shows an unflinching interest in the apocalyptic themes like the impending doom of the civilization, destruction caused by the World War II and the other wars, dehumanization, conflict between good and evil, fallen state of humanity, violence, death, murder, rootlessness, emptiness of life, poverty and squalor and seedy settings.

He is one of those writers who offer a distinctive vision or worldview just as we speak of the Dickensian world or the Kafkaesque, so Greenland is his characteristic imaginative terrain. In his writings, which spanned seventy years, he became one of the finest literary commentators on religious, cultural and political tensions in the twentieth century. He offered searching analysis to the tensions between the religious and the secular outlooks, and between political commitment and political scepticism. Paradoxes preoccupied him like the paradox of the sanctified sinner and the concept of faith without belief and the knowledge of loyalty which entails treachery. All the works taken in this book portray the stresses of modern life in numerous regions like Europe, Africa, Asia, Central and South America. Greene expresses his dissatisfaction with all these tendencies and weaves them into the matrix of a dystopic vision. The novels which have been taken in this thesis present an imaginative version of the apocalyptic end for man. Evil enslaves man, destroys his power of judgment and faculty of independent thought and makes him adopt a destructive path which finally threatens his very existence.

In Greene's war novels we get to know that man has stooped so low morally that he is reduced to a monster with no qualms of conscience. He presents in these war novels a nightmarish experience of intrigue, violence, evil and corruption. His apocalyptic imagination is satiric and dystopian here where innocent foreigners are subjected to open assaults and children are murdered mercilessly. His preoccupation with evil and the end of the world were so deep that he revealed his apocalyptic bent of mind in his secular novels in which he deals with themes like guilt, betrayal, violence, crisis and the other secular manifestations of the last loosening of Satan.

In different novels of the twentieth century, the last loosening of Satan appears in the form of images of chaos and confusion, of personal doubt and rampant hypocrisy, violence and crisis. The thesis has also argued that Greene's settings, themes and autobiographical factors portrayed in his novels are representative of the prevailing state of crisis in the world. Each of these novels represents the microcosm of the violence of a continent, obsession with betrayal, seediness, squalor, evil and corruption and apocalypse of despair.

This book also shows how Greene reveals in his novels a world of corrosion and decay, invested with evil, apparently God-forsaken. His characters live under deep psychological stress and crisis. They are prey to an obsession with evil and are tortured by a universe they cannot cope with. All of them are divided against themselves and they seem to have lost contact with the transcendental realm. They are painfully aware not only of their personal failure and the ubiquitous malaise of society but also of guilt or sin. Most of them feel the impact of violence and many of them resort to it. They are aware of being either the agents or the victims of evil. The novels discussed in this thesis dramatise their loneliness and moral failure which are symptomic of the presence of evil both in and outside their lives.

In the preceding chapters, it has also been argued that Greene faithfully renders the modern mood of anxiety and boredom and man's isolation in an alien universe. He protests against the moral and the spiritual degradation of man in our age. He also expresses his dissatisfaction with the societies in which man suffers from a feeling of estrangement and lostness caused by the complexities of modern life like mechanisation and urbanization. Like Greene all his characters seem to be sick with the different evils rampant in the contemporary society. His themes turn on the fate of individual, caught in a system and underline the horror of violence in a landscape of war, hot and cold and economic depression. His protagonists are isolated, disillusioned, defeated as if the end of the world is approaching fast.

The book has also attempted to highlight how Greene's concept of apocalypse is different from the other writers of the twentieth century. All of them share certain tendencies like the existential nature of humanity as a result of the loss of the spiritual anchor and the fact that traditional world order and the universal human essence have reached to a state of nadir or breaking point. Writers like Yeats, Eliot, Joyce, Conrad, Lawrence and Golding responded to this chaos, gloom and anxiety of the age in their own peculiar ways which has already been discussed in chapter 1. However, Greene goes a step ahead of them in that his apocalyptic vision is coloured by his childhood experiences, literary influences and Catholic imagination or sensibility. He, in an age of anti-tradtion is both traditional and modern in his approach and his apocalyptic vision fits well both in the traditional concept of the apocalypse as prophesied in *The Bible* and the secular concept of apocalypse as was done by writers like R W B Lewis, Montgomery, J R May, David Ketterer and Frank Kermode.

Bibliography

A.A. De Vitis. *Graham Greene*. Boston: Twayne Publishers, 1986.

A.D Hodder. "Emerson's Rhetoric of Revelation: Nature, the Reader, and the Apocalypse Within" *Journal of American Academy of Religion*. Pennsylvania State University Press. 1989, Vol. 60,

Albert Camus. *The Plague*. London: Stuart Gilbert, 1947.

Albert Sonnefeld. *Crossroads: Essays on the Catholic Novelists*. York SC: French Literature Publications, 1982.

Allan Ginsberg. "Playboy interview: Candid Conversation." *Playboy*. 16, 4. April 1989.

Amos N. Wilder. "Millennium and Utopia. A Study in the Background of the Idea of Progress" *The Journal of Religion*, 30, 4: 282-283. Oct., 1950.

Amos N. Wilder. "The Rhetoric of Ancient and Modern Apocalyptic." Paper read before the American Academy of Religion, 1970.

Anuradha Banerjee. *Graham Greene: Ways Of Salvation*.Ganga Kaveri Pub.House: Varanasi, 1994.

Arthur Kroker and David Cook. *The Postmodern Scene: Excremental Culture and Hyper-Aesthetics*. New York: St. Martin's Press, 1986.

B. Magee. 'Getting Along Without Doomsday.' *Horizon*: 17. Summer 1975.

Bernard Bergonzie. *A Study In Greene: Graham Greene And The Art Of The Novel*. Oxford University press: London, 2008.

Bernard Bergonzie. *Situation of the Novel*. Hermonsds worth: Penguin Books, 1972.

Brian Diemert. *Graham Greene's Thrillers And The 1930s*.Mcgill-Queen's University Press: Kingston, 1996.

Cates Baldridge. *Graham Greene's Fictions: The Virtues of Extremity*. Columbia: University of Missouri Press, 2000.

Cedric Watts. *A Preface to Greene*. Singapore. Pearson Education, 2003.

Daniel Wojcik. *The End of the World As We Know It: Faith, Fatalism and Apocalypse in America*. New York: New York University Press, 1997.

David Ketterer: *New Worlds for Old*: Bloomington and London: Indian University Press, 1974.

David Lodge. *Introduction to Francois Mauriac: The Viper's Rangle*. New York: Carroll & Graf, 1987.

David Pryce-Jones. *Graham Greene*. London: Oliver & Boyd, 1963.

Dermot Gilvary. *Dangerous Edges Of Graham Greene: Journeys With Saints And Sinners*. Continuum: UK, 2011

Ellis Hanson. *Decadence and Catholicism*. Cambridge MA: Harvard University Press, 1997.

Eric Fromm. *The Present Human Condition: Modern Essays*. Ed. Russel Nye. Illinois. Scott. Foresman and Company, 1963.

Frank Kermode. *The Sense of an Ending*. London: Oxford Univ. Press, 1970.

Gene Kellogg. *The Vital Tradition: The Catholic Novel in a Period of Convergence*. Chicago: Loyola University Press, 1970.

George Turner. *Down There in Darkness*. New York: Doherty Associates, 2000.

George Watson. 'The Empire of Lionel Trilling', *Sewanee Review*. The John Hopkins University Press, 1927.

Graham Greene. 'At Home'. *Collected Essays*. London: Bodley Head, 1981.

Graham Greene. "The Gamble" in *Babbling April*. Oxford: Blackwell, 1952.

Graham Greene. "The Lost Childhood" in *The Lost Childhood and Other Essays*. London: Eyre & Spottiswoode, 1951.

Graham Greene. *A Burnt-Out Case*. London: Heinemann, 1961.

Graham Greene. *A Gun For Sale*. London: Heinemann, 1936.

Graham Greene. *A Sort of Life*. New York: Simon and Schuster, 1971.

Graham Greene. *Articles Of Faith: The Collected Tablet Journalism Of Graham Greene, 1936 - 1987*.Signal Books Lyd: Oxford, 2006.

Graham Greene. *Brighton Rock*. London: Heinemann, 1938.

Graham Greene. *Collected Essays*. London: Bodley Head, 1969.

Graham Greene. *Journey without Maps*. London: Heinemann, 1936.

Graham Greene. *Notes on the Way: Time and Tide*. 1940.

Graham Greene. *Reflections*. London: Reinhardt, 1990.

Graham Greene. *Rumour at Nightfall*. London: Heinemarm, 1931.

Graham Greene. *Stamboul Train*. London: Heinemann, 1932.

Graham Greene. *The Comedians*. London: Bodely Head, 1966.

Graham Greene. *The Confidential Agent*. London: Heinemann, 1939.

Graham Greene. *The End of the Affair*. London: Heinemann. 1951.

Graham Greene. *The Human Factor*. London: Bodley Head, 1978.

Graham Greene. *The Lawless Roads*. London: Longman, 1939.

Graham Greene. *The Lost Childhood & Other Essays*. London: Barnes & Noble 1951.

Graham Greene. *The Ministry of Fear*. London: Heinemann, 1943.

Graham Greene. *The Name of Action*. New York: Dombleday, 1931.

Graham Greene. *The Power and the Glory*. London: Heinemannm, 1940.

Graham Greene. *The Quiet American*. London: Heinemann, 1955.

Graham Greene. *The Tenth Man*. London: Bodely Head and Anthony Blond, 1985.

Graham Greene. *Ways of Escape*. London: Bodely Head, 1980.

Haim Gordon, Hayim Gordon. *Fighting Evil: Unsung Heroes In The Novels Of Graham Greene*.Praeger Publishers: Westport, 1997.

Harold Bloom. *Anxiety of Influence*. London: Oxford University Press, 1973.

Harold Rosenbarg. *The Tradition of the New*. New York: Horizon Press, 1959.

J Adamson. *Graham Greene: The Dangerous Edge: Where Art And Politics Meet*. Palgrave Macmillan: UK, 1990.

J. Eric Hobsbawm. *Primitive Rebels: Studies in Archaic Forms of Social Movement in the Nineteenth and Twentieth Centuries*. New York: Norton, 1965.

J. Hillis Miller's The *Disappearance of God: Five Nineteenth Century Writers*. London: John Murray, 1952.

J. P. Kulshrestha, Graham *Greene: The Novelist*. Palgrave Macmillan: UK, 1979.

J.G. Melton. *Cults, Religion and Violence*. New York: Cambridge University Press, 2002.

J.J. Collins. In Craig A. Evans & Stanly Porter (eds). *Apocalypse Literature: Dictionary of Newter. Backgrounds*. Downers Grove Il., Intervarsity Press, 2004.

James Noxon. "Kieregard's Stages & A Burnt out Case." *Review of English Literature*, 3, 1962.

Jerry H. Bryant. *The Open Decision*. London: The Free Press, 1970.

John Atkins. *Graham Greene*. London: Calder & Boyars, 1957.

John Henry Newman. *Apologia Pro Vita Sua*. London: J.M. Dent & Sons Ltd, 1864.

John Kenneth Galbraith. *The Anatomy of Power*. Boston: Houghton Mifflin Co, 1983.

John Lehman. *New Writing*. London: Penguin New Writing, 1944.

John Maddox. *The Doomsday Syndrome*. New York: Mc Gram Hill Book Company, 1972.

John R. May. *Toward A New Earth*. London: University of Notre Dame Press, 1972.

John Whalen-Bridge. *The Apocalyptic Complex–Origins, Histories*. Urbana: University of Illinois Press, 2001.

Joseph Pearce. "The Unquiet Graham Greene" *The American Conservative*, October 22, 2007.

Karl Mannheism. *Diagonosis of Our Time*. New York: New York University Press, 1944.

Kenneth L. Woodward, Angus Deming, and Judith Gingold. "Apocalypse Chic." *Newsweek*. 17 Feb, 1975.

Keshava Prasad. *Graham Greene: The Human Predicament*. New Delhi: Adhyayan, 2008

Malcolm Bradbury in *A Dictionary of Modern Critical Terms*, ed. Roger Fowler. Routledge & Kegan Paul, 1987.

Marie Beatrice Mesnet. *Graham Greene and the Heart of the Matter*. London: Cresset Press, 1954.

Marie Francoise Allian. *The Other Man: Conservations with Graham Greene*. London: Bodley, 1983.

Mary Gerhart and Anthony C. Yu. "Morphologies of Faith" *Essays in religion and Culture*. Atlanta GA: Scholars Press, 1990, p. 181-201.

Mary Shelley. *Frankenstein*. Lackington: Hughes, Harding, Mavor & Jones, 1818.

Mary Shelley. *The Last Man*. Lincoln, Neb University of Nebraska Press. 1965.

Michael Barkum. Crucible of the Millennium: *The Burned Over District*. New York: Syracuse University Press, 1986.

Michael Barkun. *Disaster & the Millenium*. New Haven: Yale University Press, 1974.

Mircea Eliade. *Images and Symbols*. New York: Sheed & Ward, 1952.

Morton Dauwen Zabel. *Graham Greene: The Best and the Worst in Craft and Character*. London: Gollancz, 1957.

Murray Roston. *Graham Greene's Narrative Strategies: A Study Of The Major Novels*. Palgrave Macmillan: UK, 2006.

Northop Frye. *Anatomy of Criticism*.Princeton: Princeton Univ. Press. 1957.

Oswald Spengler. *Decline of the West*. Michigan: Farmington Hills. 1981.

Padmaker Mishra. *Graham Greene: Philosopher – Thriller-Writer*.Omsons Publications: New Delhi, 2005.

Paul Brains. *Nuclear Holocausts: Atomic War in Fiction Kent*. OH: Kant State University Press, 1987.

Paul Tillich. *On Art and Architecture*. New York: Cross Road, 1987.

Peter Mudford. *Graham Greene.* Northolt House: Devon, 1996

R. Buckminster Fuller. *Utopia or Oblivion: The Prospects for Humanity.* New York: Bantam Books Inc, 1972.

R.W.B. Lewis. *"Days of Wrath & laughter", Trials of the Word.* New Haven: Yale University Press, 1966.

Richard A. Falk. *This Endangered Planet.* New York: Viatage Books, 1972.

Richard Dellamora. *Post modern Apocalypse. Theory and Cultural Practice at the End.* Philadelphia: University of Pennsylvania Press, 1995.

Richard Hoggert. *Auden: An Introductory Essay.* London: Chatto & Windus, 1951.

Richard Tarnas. *The Passion of the Western Mind: Understanding the Ideas that have Shaped our World.* New York: Bellantine, 1991.

Robert Alter. 'The Apocalyptic temper.' *In Commentary* June, 1966.

Robert Detweiler. *Breaking the Fall: Religious Readings of Contemporary Fiction.* San Francisco. Harper & Row, 1989.

Robert L. Gale. *Characters and Plots In The Fiction Of Graham Greene.* McFarland and Company: Jefferson, 2006.

Robert O. Evans. *Graham Greene: Some Critical Considerations.* University Press of Kentucky: Lexington, 2009.

Robert Pendleton. *Graham Greene's Conradian Masterplot.* New York: St. Martin's Press, 1996.

Robert Pendleton. *Graham Greene's Conradian Masterplot.* New York: St Martin's Press 1996.

Robert Scheer. *Why We Don't Know Our Enemy.* Online: Truth Dig. Com, 2006.

Robert W. Brockway. *Myth from the Ice Age to Mickey Mouse.* Albang State University of New York Press, 1937.

Samuel V. T and Brian Moore. *Religious Paradigms In The Novels Of Graham Greene*. Discovery Publishing House: New Delhi, 2011.

Sir Compton Mackenzie. *Sinister*. London, Arkham House, 1967.

Stephen K. Land. *The Human Imperative: A Study Of The Novels Of Graham Greene (AMS Studies In Modern Literature)*. Ams Press: Brooklyn, 2006.

Terry Eagleton. "Relucant Heroes: The Novels of Graham Greene" in *Graham Greene Modern Critical Views*. New York: Chelsea House, 1987.

Theodore P. Fraser. *The Modern Catholic Novel in Europe*. New York: Macmillan, 1994.

Urbashi Barat. *Graham Greene: A Study Of His Novelistic Development*.Classical Publishing Company: New Delhi, 1995.

Veronica Hellinger. *Future/Present: The End of Science Fiction*. Berlin: Ulrich Ammon, 1996.

W. Warren Wagar. *A Short History of the Future*. Chicago: University of Chicago Press, 1989.

Whitsun and Brewer. *Nearing the End*. Urbana: University of Illinois Press, 1989.

William Golding. *Lord of the Flies*. London: Faber and Faber, 1954.

William Shakespeare. *Hamlet*. London: Cambridge University Press.

Zbigniew Lewqicki. *The Bang and the Whimper: Apocalypse and Entropy in American Literature*. Westport: Greenwood Press, 1984.

Index

G

H

I

J

K

L

M

N

O

Adhyayan
9